Jeremy Taylor, John Dennis

Jeremy Taylor's golden Sayings

Jeremy Taylor, John Dennis

Jeremy Taylor's golden Sayings

ISBN/EAN: 9783743314122

Manufactured in Europe, USA, Canada, Australia, Japa

Cover: Foto ©ninafisch / pixelio.de

Manufactured and distributed by brebook publishing software (www.brebook.com)

Jeremy Taylor, John Dennis

Jeremy Taylor's golden Sayings

JEREMY TAYLOR'S
GOLDEN SAYINGS.

EDITED WITH AN INTRODUCTION

BY

JOHN DENNIS,

AUTHOR OF "STUDIES IN ENGLISH LITERATURE," ETC.

London:

A. D. INNES & CO.,

31 & 32, BEDFORD STREET, STRAND.

1893.

PREFACE.

JEREMY TAYLOR belongs to the select band of authors who have a life beyond life. Every critic of our great prose writers mentions his name with honour; every student of our literature knows that he is the most eloquent and one of the most erudite of English divines. The titles at least of his principal works are familiar to most readers, and no doubt there are still many devout souls who feed with delight in the green pastures of his "Holy Living" and "Holy Dying."

Probably this is the utmost popularity that can now be claimed for Taylor. The greatest poets use a universal language upon which time has no power; the ear is never closed to their music, the heart will always respond to their charm. Poetry of the highest order cannot grow obsolete, and time has had no influence on Homer and Dante, on Shakespeare and on Milton. The prose writer, on the other hand, is at a disadvantage; and the few that after the lapse of many years retain their full vitality, do so for the most part through perfection of style and by thoughts borne on the wings of imagination—the very qualities that are most akin to poetry. Perfection of style cannot be claimed for Jeremy Taylor, but the magic of style may be, and he has also an inexhaustible wealth of language. Of all our prose writers on serious subjects he has the liveliest fancy and perhaps the sweetest turns of expression. Of this I am sure, that the more we dig in his mine the more gold shall we extract, and the more shall we be conscious of the depth as well as fertility of his genius. The exuberance of his fancy is never an indication of poverty of thought. The most poetical of divines is assuredly also one of the weightiest. If he rambles to pluck flowers by the way, he has always the cunning art of extracting from them medicine or fragrance.

Knowing a little of Taylor's great and versatile powers, I feel how inadequate any gleanings from so illustrious an author must be—inadequate, but not, I trust, ill-judged. Whatever makes such a writer better known must be of some service to his memory, and, which he would have desired far more, may prove of benefit to readers unacquainted with the fifteen volumes whence these "Golden Sayings" are extracted. This is the editor's aim, and will be regarded, it may be hoped, as a justification of this selection.

INTRODUCTION.

JEREMY TAYLOR was born at Cambridge in 1613. The day of his birth is uncertain, but he was baptised on the 15th of August in that year. His father, Nathaniel Taylor, a barber in the town, was, to quote his son's words, "reasonably learned," and boasted his descent from Dr. Rowland Taylor, the well-known martyr, who died at the stake in the third year of Queen Mary, "with a courageous and kindly cheerfulness which has scarcely its parallel even in those days of religious heroism."[1] At the age of thirteen Jeremy entered Caius College as a sizar, a humble position which enabled many a poor student to gain a university education. Twelve months before, John Milton, then in his seventeenth year, had gone up to

[1] Heber's "Life of Jeremy Taylor," p. 4.

Christ's. The greatest poet and the most eloquent divine of that age might therefore have been friends in youth, but neither at that early period, nor in later days, do these two illustrious men appear to have met, and there is not even an allusion in the works of one to the writings of the other. Their opinions were, it has been justly said, in direct opposition, and yet in many respects the iconoclast and the Laudian divine were kindred spirits, loving what is beautiful, aiming at what is pure and lofty, ardent upholders of what they deemed the right, and eager in the pursuit of knowledge.

In 1631 Taylor took his bachelor's degree, some time later he gained a fellowship and was soon afterwards ordained, having previously received his degree of Master of Arts. Handsome in form and face, eloquent and earnest, the youthful clergyman preached in St. Paul's, and was taken, to quote the high-flown language of his friend Dr. Rust, "for some young angel newly descended from the visions of glory." Laud regarded the sermon as "beyond exception and beyond imitation; yet the wise prelate thought him too young, but the youth humbly begged his Grace to pardon that fault, and promised if he lived he would amend it."[1]

By the Archbishop's advice Taylor removed to Oxford, where, in 1635, he was admitted Master of Arts in University College, and in January, 1636 —a month and a year made memorable in English history by Hampden's refusal to pay the tax of ship money—he was appointed Fellow of All Soul's. In 1637 he was presented to the Rectory of Uppingham, and Laud, bent eagerly on his advancement, obtained for him the position of Chaplain to King Charles. Then we are told of his marriage, in 1639, to Phoebe Langsdale, the daughter of a widow lady in the town, and how, on giving birth to her third child in 1642, the mother and infant died, and were buried on the same day. This grievous loss happened when Taylor was in his thirtieth year.

The seventeenth century was not, like the nineteenth, an age of biographers, and its most distinguished men lived and died with little notice from the press. Of Taylor's life the bare facts are recorded, but detail, which is the salt of biography, is almost wholly lacking. This is the

[1] Rust's Funeral Sermon.

more to be deplored because Taylor not only ranks with the most distinguished of English authors, but was also closely associated with the public events of the time. He had the misfortune to live in an age of political upheaval and of ecclesiastical strife—an age in which it seemed as though the old paths would be obliterated and the ancient landmarks swept away. As chaplain to the King, Taylor had now to share his fortunes. It is by no means easy to trace his movements, but we know that he accompanied the Royal army, and in 1643 was present at the battle of Newbury, in which Falkland lost his life. At the siege of the Castle of Cardigan, in 1644, the Royalists were repulsed, and Taylor was taken prisoner; but the imprisonment could not have lasted long, since before the end of the year he was at Oxford. The warfare he was called upon to wage was with the pen. In that period of conflict it was impossible that a captain so well armed and so strong in what he deemed the righteousness of a great cause should decline to go into the battle. In 1643 Taylor had published "Episcopacy Asserted," and now the University Press issued his "Defence of the Liturgy," a work of practical value at a time when the public services of the Church were not tolerated and the Book of Common Prayer openly burnt.

The year in which he was deprived of his living by the committee appointed in 1640 for ejecting "scandalous ministers" appears to be uncertain, but if a Royalist newspaper of the day may be trusted,[1] Taylor's successor, a man of the name of Isaac Massey, was at once scandalous and profane. "The successor of Taylor," says Willmott, "was probably a brother of the Colonel Massey who occupies so prominent a place in the revolutionary memorials of Whitelock, and whose sacrilegious exploits in Gloucestershire long preserved his memory in that county. He stripped churches with more than ordinary enthusiasm; selling communion-plate and tearing up prayer-books; while the soldiers wore the surplices over their arms. Of such a person the brawler at Uppingham would be the appropriate deputy."[2]

When Taylor married a second time we do not know, but the lady's name, Joanna Bridges, has

---

[1] *Mercurius Aulicus*, May 2, 1644.
[2] "Bishop Jeremy Taylor, his Predecessors, Contemporaries, and Successors," p. 108.

been preserved. She is said to have been a beautiful woman, and "is generally believed," Bishop Heber states, "to be a natural daughter of Charles I. when Prince of Wales, and under the guidance of the dissipated and licentious Buckingham." The lady was the owner of Mandinnam, a good estate near Llangadock, in Carmarthenshire. Her husband, however, appears to have derived little benefit from it, for, like John Milton, he was forced to keep a school, at which, according to Anthony Wood, "several youths were most loyally educated and afterwards sent to the Universities." Llanvihangel Aberbythic, the scene of his labours in South Wales, is not far from Grongar Hill, of which Dyer has sung the praises, and it is close to Golden Grove, the seat of Taylor's friends, the Earl and Countess of Carbery, whose names will be honoured as long as the great divine whom they befriended is loved and reverenced. The name of the earl's estate, it will be remembered, is the title given by Taylor to his "Choice Manual" of "what is to be believed, practised, and desired, or prayed for," and it was amidst scenes of pastoral loveliness, and in the enjoyment of a friendship which he has worthily commemorated, that his best and most popular works were written. These were Taylor's happiest days, and the brief respite from care which he enjoyed in this pleasant exile seems to be reflected in the following passage :—

"I am fallen into the hands of publicans and sequestrators, and they have taken all from me; what now? Let me look about me. They have left me the sun and moon, fire and water, a loving wife, and many friends to pity me, and some to relieve me, and I can still discourse; and, unless I list, they have not taken away my merry countenance and my cheerful spirit and a good conscience; they still have left me the providence of God and all the promises of the gospel, and my religion, and my hopes of heaven, and my charity to them too; and still I sleep and digest, I eat and drink, I read and meditate; I can walk in my neighbours' pleasant fields, and see the variety of natural beauties, and delight in all that in which God delights—that is in virtue and wisdom, in the whole creation, and in God Himself. And he that has so many causes of joy and so great, is very much in love with sorrow and peevishness, who loses all these pleasures, and chooses to sit down upon his little handful of thorns." Taylor adds, with the love of grotesque illustration that characterises many of his most serious passages: "Such a person is fit to bear Nero company in his funeral sorrow for the loss of one of Poppea's hairs, or help to mourn for Lesbia's sparrow."[1]

In 1647 appeared his great work, "The Liberty of Prophesying," a plea for toleration in an age in which that virtue was not understood, or, if accepted by a few far-sighted men as a theory, was rendered impracticable by the condition of the time. Taylor admitted that if an opinion was liable to disturb the public peace it became a question of policy and not a question of religion. "Only those governments," Dr. Gardiner writes, "which have a sense of their own security will grant liberty of association as well as liberty of opinion, and it was the want of this sense of security which made complete toleration impossible in the crisis through which the nation was passing."[2] Cromwell has been praised for permitting every form of dissent that was not associated, like the creed of the Levellers, with political

---

[1] "Holy Living," c. 11.
[2] "The History of the Great Civil War," vol. iii. p. 138.

anarchy, but his position never allowed him to exhibit the slightest tolerance for the Church of England or for that of Rome. While asserting that liberty of conscience was a natural right, he found it a belief too perilous to practise.

Many judgments have been passed upon the " Liberty of Prophesying," but it is enough to say here that Coleridge read the book with the warmest admiration, and that Hallam, while pointing out its inconsistencies, calls it " the first famous plea in this country for tolerance in religion on a comprehensive basis and on deep-seated foundations." Here, as elsewhere, Taylor's enormous learning and discursive fancy are more conspicuous than his logic or consistency, but he is never inconsistent in his love of what is noble and true, in the largeness of his sympathies, and in the strength of his affections. After alluding to the persecuting spirit of the age, and pointing out that there was no cure for it but piety and charity, he adds :—

" All these mischiefs proceed not from this, that all men are not of one mind, for that is neither necessary nor possible, but that every opinion is made an article of faith, every article is the ground of a quarrel, every quarrel makes a faction, every faction is zealous, and all zeal pretends for God, and whatsoever is for God cannot be too much. We by this time are come to that pass, we think we love not God except we hate our brother; and we have not the virtue of religion unless we persecute all religions but our own; for lukewarmness is so odious to God and man, that we, proceeding furiously upon these mistakes, by supposing we preserve the body, we destroy the soul of religion; or by being zealous for faith, or, which is all one, for that which we mistake for faith, we are cold in charity, and so lose the reward of both."

It is interesting to observe that the opinions urged by Jeremy Taylor when the Church he loved so dearly had fallen on evil days, were held by him as strongly when the Restoration had once more made Episcopacy dominant. In a sermon preached before the members of the Irish Parliament in 1661, he says:—

"Whatever you do, let not the pretence of a different religion make you think it lawful to oppress any man in his just rights; for not opinions, but laws, and doing as we would be done to, are the measures of justice. And though justice does alike to all men, Jew and Christian, Lutheran and Calvinist, yet to do right to them that are of another opinion is the way to win them. But if you for conscience' sake do them wrong, they will hate both you and your religion."[1]

This was the fruitful season of Taylor's life, and a year after the publication of the " Liberty of Prophesying," he produced "The Great Exemplar." The work is not in any degree critical, but is intended for the devout reader who desires not to question but to love. Unfortunately there is much in the book which does not tend to devotion in an age like ours, for the author, in order to enforce his arguments, makes use of the most extravagant legends as well as of the New Testament, and appears to place legend and history on the same level. But the beauty and wholesome piety of the narrative are beyond all praise. It is

[1] It has been doubted whether Taylor's conduct as a bishop was in accordance with these liberal sentiments, for he is said upon his first visitation to have declared thirty-six churches vacant, of which forcible possession was taken by his orders. The fact, if it be one, is not mentioned by Heber, but he observes that in the Bishop's diocese more than in any other part of Ireland, "the clearance of the episcopal clergy had been most effectual, and their places supplied by the sturdiest champions of the covenant." To vindicate and uphold Episcopacy amidst opponents such as these could have been no easy task.

rich in wise suggestions, in tender episodes, in lovely pictures, and in earnest counsels with regard to the duties of daily life. Taylor, although one of the most imaginative prose writers in the language, is the most practical of divines, and delights in dwelling on the homeliest duties. This he does constantly, and with a winning charm, in "The Great Exemplar." There is in this, as in nearly all his writings, what Bishop Heber calls "grave trifling," but the intense seriousness of the writer's purpose is not affected by it. The book became popular at once, and has retained a measure of popularity ever since. He was encouraged by its success to produce " The Rules of Holy Living and of Holy Dying "—two treatises which, although published separately, form one work. It is probably the best known manual of the kind in the language, and beyond comparison the most eloquent. The splendour of Taylor's rhetoric, the wealth of his imagery, the persuasiveness of his piety, and the frequent lapses of taste which mar his genius, may be said to reach their high-water mark in these " Rules." Truly does Hazlitt say that the " Holy Living and Dying " is a divine pastoral. The living power of the book has been felt by many. It so influenced John Wesley in his college days as to change the current of his life, and it is interesting to remember that it soothed the dying hours of John Keats. Practical counsels for the religious life were rare in days when the press teemed with pamphlets on Election, Reprobation, and Final Perseverance. Theology in Taylor's judgment, was "rather a divine life than a divine knowledge." "In heaven," he writes, "we shall first see and then love; but here on earth we must love, and love will open our eyes as well as our hearts, and we shall then see and perceive and understand."

It was at Golden Grove, under the protection of Lord Carbery, that Taylor published his Sermons, some of which, like "The Marriage Ring," are still familiar to his readers. When the second Lady Carbery died Taylor celebrated her virtues and piety in an elaborate discourse adorned (or deformed), after the fashion of the age, with Greek and Latin quotations, and containing a few passages in which, as in the following quotation, prose seems to tread upon the verge of poetry: "In all her religion and in all her acts of relation towards God, she had a strange evenness and untroubled passage, sliding towards her ocean of God and of infinity with a certain and silent motion." The lady's successor—for the Earl married a third time—was Alice, the eighth daughter of the first Earl of Bridgewater, who has the rare distinction of having her name linked to that of Jeremy Taylor and of Milton. It was to celebrate her father's entry on his high office of Lord President of Wales that "Comus" was written, and Alice, then a girl in her teens, was the "Lady" in that incomparably beautiful Masque. To her, years later, as Lady Carbery, Taylor dedicated Part III. of "The Great Exemplar," the first edition having been dedicated to "the very dear and excellent person" to whom she was the successor. The task was one of delicacy, but he performed it with a skilful hand.

Again and again the student is baffled who attempts to follow consecutively the course of Taylor's life. Much is left to conjecture, and the events that can be traced with certainty are so isolated as to be often barren of interest. According to John Evelyn's diary, he was preaching in London in 1654, and in the following year Evelyn records how he heard him preach again, conferred with him about some spiritual matters, and used him thenceforward as his "ghostly father." Then, as we learn from a letter of Evelyn's, Taylor suffered a short imprisonment in Chepstow Castle —the second which he had to undergo—and it seems to have been due to the vigorous defence of the Church of England in his Preface to the Golden Grove.[1] This was in what Isaac Walton calls "the dangerous year," for it was then that the Episcopal clergy were prohibited from exercising any part of their ministerial functions or from acting as schoolmasters. In the course of this year Taylor published his "Unum Necessarium ; or the Doctrine and Practice of Repentance," a book which created much controversy and provoked many replies.

A visit to London and to Evelyn's home at Sayes Court took place in 1656, and there he met, as we learn from the Diary, " that excellent person and great virtuoso," Robert Boyle. Some weeks were spent in London, where Taylor had a strong desire to live, and was only hindered, as he wrote afterwards,

[1] Taylor's third and last imprisonment was in 1658. He was confined in the Tower "on account of the indiscretion of his bookseller, Royston, who had prefixed to his 'Collection of offices' a print of Christ in the attitude of prayer."

by the *res angusta domi*. "I am much persuaded," he writes, "that by my abode in the voisinage of London I may receive advantages of society and books to enable me better to serve God and the interest of souls." At the end of the letter he informs Evelyn of the death of a child in these quaintly pathetic words: "Dear Sir,—I am in some little disorder by reason of the death of a little child of mine, a boy that lately made us very glad; but now he rejoices in his little orb while we think and sigh and long to be as safe as he is." Not many months later family sorrow reached him again; he buried "two sweet, hopeful boys," and adds, to the perplexity of his biographers, that he had now but one son left. Lady Wray, Bishop Taylor's granddaughter, distinctly states, however, that two sons lived to manhood, and that their mother died at Uppingham; but it has been suggested that "it is more reasonable to conclude that the granddaughter may have confused the number of her uncles than that the father could have forgotten one of his sons.[1] Bishop Heber suggests a solution of the difficulty. "These are points," he says, "in which she could hardly have

[1] Willmott's "Jeremy Taylor," p. 163.

been mistaken, and I know no better or more probable way of reconciling them to this letter than by supposing that the two sons by his first wife were at this time separated from him and with their mother's family, and that the children whose death he laments, as well as the surviving son . . . who appears to have been afterwards buried at Lisburn, in Ireland, were the fruits of his second marriage. It is strange, however, that he speaks of the son who was with him as his *only one;* and it is strange, whichever hypothesis we adopt, that he does not say anything of his daughters, and that in none of the letters which are preserved, is any direct mention made of either of his wives." [1]

A grant of a pension from his generous friend Evelyn gave Taylor more freedom than he had hitherto enjoyed. "I know it is more blessed to give than to receive," he writes, "and yet as I noways repine at the Providence that forces me to receive, so neither can I envy that felicity of yours, not only that you can but that you do give." No one understood better the felicities of friendship, and about this time he wrote his essay

[1] Heber's "Taylor," vol. i. p. 64.

on the subject and dedicated it to "the matchless Orinda" Katharine Philips, whose name, unsupported by her own poetry, lives in Jeremy Taylor's prose and in the elegaic verses of Cowley. Taylor was at this time preparing for the press his book on Casuistry, and seems to have paid several visits to London in order, no doubt, to consult the authorities needed in so laborious an undertaking.

The "Ductor Dubitantium" is styled by Hallam the most extensive and learned work on the subject in the English language, but he observes that it exhibits the author's characteristic defects and that his solution of moral problems is often unsatisfactory. It was Taylor's most arduous achievement, and may be said to stand apart from his other works, not in the matter only, but in the style, which is free for the most part from the luxuriance of imagery in which he so often delights elsewhere. There are passages in the work worthy of the greatest masters of English prose, but the subject has lost its interest, and the "Ductor Dubitantium" ranks with the dead works to be found in every large library which are rarely taken from the shelves to be consulted, and never to be read.

INTRODUCTION.

In London Taylor met Lord Conway, who offered him a lectureship at Lisburn and a home at Portmore, about nine miles distant on the borders of Lough Neagh. Taylor's first impression of the proposal was unfavourable. "I like not," he writes to Evelyn, "the condition of being a lecturer under the dispose of another. . . . Sir, the stipend is so inconsiderable it will not pay the charge of removing myself and family. It is wholly arbitrary, for the triers may overthrow it or the vicar may forbid it, or the subscribers may die, or grow weary, or be absent." The invitation was therefore declined; but, moved probably by fresh arguments in its favour, Taylor afterwards accepted the offer, and apparently in the early summer of 1658 left London for Ireland. Thence, a year later, he writes to Evelyn of the pleasantness of his retreat, and relates how he is engaged in completing his "Rule of Conscience," but he adds: "I fear my peace in Ireland is likely to be short, for a Presbyterian and a madman have informed against me as a dangerous man to their religion, and for using the sign of the cross in baptism. The worst event of the information which I fear is my return into England, which, although I am not desirous it should be upon these terms, yet if it be without much violence I shall not be much troubled."

Taylor's fear was well founded. On August 11, 1659, a warrant of the Irish Privy Council issued to the Governor of Carrickfergus, required him immediately to "cause the body of Jeremy Taylor to be sent up to Dublin under safe custody." Strange to say the warrant was not enforced until the winter of the following year. "I had been," he writes, "in the worst of our winter weather sent for to Dublin by our late Anabaptist Commissioners, and found the evil of it so great that in my going I began to be ill; but in my return had my ill redoubled." There was no imprisonment this time, and the inconvenience of a long journey and some temporary indisposition were comparatively light trials. Taylor regained his health on the return of spring, and then on visiting London he found his fortunes changed. Cromwell, it will be remembered, had died in September, 1658, and in April, 1660, Taylor added his signature to the declaration which led to the return of Charles II. Five weeks later he was on the throne, and in June the "Ductor Dubitantium" was published and inscribed to the King. That such a work should be dedicated to such a monarch was the irony of fate. Happily Taylor was not neglected in the distribution of the rewards bestowed upon the Royalists. On the 6th of August he was appointed to the bishopric of Down and Connor, and a little later he was elected Vice-Chancellor of Dublin University. " Honours and preferment," Heber writes, " were now flowing fast upon him. In February he was made a member of the Irish Privy Council, and on the 30th of April, in addition to his former diocese, he was entrusted with the administration of the small adjacent one of Dromore on account, in the words of the writ under the privy seal, ' of his virtue, wisdom, and industry.'"[1]

His duties as a bishop were far from light. Taylor loved peace, and his misfortunes, it has been truly said, " had only served to mellow his sweet and harmonious temper"; but the staunch upholders of the Covenant were rampant in the land and the peace for which he strove seemed impossible. The Covenant bound the men who signed it to extirpate prelacy; how, then, could

[1] Heber, vol. i., p. 103.

they tolerate a bishop who had written strongly in its defence? Taylor's persuasive efforts, however, were not without effect. By degrees he won the laity over to his side, and was also on a friendly footing with some of the ministers. Unaltered probably in opinion, they yielded in some degree to the bishop's gentleness and charity.

In the first year of his episcopate Taylor lost his son Edward, who was buried at Lisburn. Two months later the Irish Parliament was opened, and the bishop preached an eloquent sermon on the occasion before the Lords and Commons in St. Patrick's Cathedral. In 1664 he published his " Dissuasive from Popery," a treatise that abounds with the marks of his characteristic style. It was not received in silence, and Taylor replied to the arguments of his opponents by the publication of a " Second Part." In the same year he wrote to the Archbishop of Canterbury, begging that if his Grace did not wish him to die prematurely he might be removed to an English bishopric, as the country no longer agreed with his health. Since his promotion he had continued to live in the neighbourhood of Portmore, where he had many friends, and now a large income enabled him to exercise the hospitality and the charity which must have been especially pleasing to a man of his generous nature after so many years of poverty. Bishoprics are not to be had for the asking, and what reply Taylor received from the Archbishop of Canterbury we do not know; but the application led to no result, and the few remaining years of Taylor's life were spent in Ireland. He died from a fever at Lisburn on the 13th of August, 1667—a year distinguished by the publication of "Paradise Lost"—in the fifty-fifth year of his age, leaving a wife and three daughters behind him. Of two sons by his first wife one is said to have died in a duel, while the second, who had been intended for Holy Orders, became a favourite companion of the Duke of Buckingham, and died of decline about a fortnight before the death of his father. It may be added that Dr. Rust, who afterwards succeeded Taylor in the diocese, celebrated his friend's virtues in a style more remarkable for profuse rhetoric than for good taste. The praise which, in a funeral sermon, he heaps upon the bishop is so great that it becomes ridiculous, but there is one brief passage in his eulogy which is likely to be true: "His soul," he says, "was made up of harmony, and he never spake but he charmed his hearer ... his very tone and cadences were strangely musical."

All the works of Jeremy Taylor are either polemical or distinctly religious. He is one of the most devout and one of the most practical of Church of England divines, but in his theological views he is often inconsistent and illogical, and on some points of dogma has been pronounced unsound. None, however, of Bishop Taylor's opponents have ever questioned his singleness of purpose, his intense sincerity, and the noble elevation of character that lifted him above the smoke and stir of the controversies amidst which it was his lot to live. Those who knew Taylor

> "felt how awful goodness is, and saw
> Virtue in her shape how lovely,"

and many a reader of his works has felt and seen it also. "What a man he is!" writes Edward Fitzgerald; "he has such a knowledge of the nature of man and such powers of expressing its properties, that I sometimes feel as if he had had some exact counterpart of my own individual character under his eye when he lays open the

depths of the heart or traces sin to its root. The
eye of his portrait expresses this keen intuition,
and I think I should less like to have stood with
a lie on my tongue before him than before any
other I know of." [1]

And Taylor is one of the glories of English
literature. His faults of style are obvious, but
they are the faults of a man of genius. His vast
erudition, his inexhaustible fancy, his love of
quaint illustrations, and an irresistible propensity
to wander wherever fancy might lead him, tend
sometimes to a prodigality of words. He loses
his argument in rhetoric and blends the solemnity
of his appeals with grotesque allusions. He sails
his ship occasionally without a compass, and his
passengers find themselves unexpectedly upon
strange waters. The leaden weight of some
theological writers, however, would sink any ship,
but Taylor's barque is always buoyant and is
certain to carry us at last into a happy haven.
The defects of a mind like his can therefore
readily be pardoned, and they are slight when
weighed against the strength of intellect and the
exquisite beauty of thought that give vitality to

---

[1] E. Fitzgerald's "Letters," vol. i. p. 29.

his works. It is as a writer of earnest thoughtfulness and deep piety that Taylor has gained the sympathy and affection which still secure to him a home in many Christian hearts. He was a controversialist by the accident of the time. To his gentle, loving spirit, discord in the region where peace is most needed must have been painful indeed. He did not shun discussion nor bate a jot of confidence in the soundness of his position, but it was in green pastures and by still waters that he loved best to wander. The voice of song was sweeter to him than the conflict of arms, the shepherd's crook than the spear.

Every attempt to imitate Taylor has resulted in failure, for style, as Wordsworth happily said, is not the dress of thought, but the incarnation of thought. "Taylor's periods," Coleridge writes, "have been frequently attempted by his admirers; you may, perhaps, just catch the turn of a simile or single image, but to write in the real manner of Jeremy Taylor would require as mighty a mind as his."

It is one aim of the present selection to show that Taylor is not a slave to what may be called his characteristic style, and that in addition to pages distinguished by rhetoric, by teeming fancy and by poetical imagination, his works abound with weighty thoughts expressed in language as simple as it is precise. It would be difficult indeed to select from the writings of any of our old divines more laconic sayings than are to be found in Taylor's works. And it may be doubted whether there is one of them, unless it be Hooker, who gives the reader such an impression of intellectual capacity.

JEREMY TAYLOR'S GOLDEN SAYINGS.

FALSE ARGUMENTS.

HE that proves a certain truth from an uncertain argument, is like him that wears a wooden leg, when he hath two sound legs already; it hinders his going, but helps him not: the truth of God stands not in need of such supporters. Sermons: "Funeral of the Lord Primate."

CUMULATIVE ARGUMENTS.

Probable arguments are like little stars, every one of which will be useless as to our conduct and enlightening; but when they are tied together by order and vicinity, by the finger of God and the hand of an angel, they make a constellation, and are not only powerful in their influence, but like a bright angel, to guide and to "Ductor Dubitantium," book i. c. iv.

enlighten our way. And although the light is not great as the light of the sun or moon, yet mariners sail by their conduct; and though with trepidation and some danger, yet very regularly they enter into the haven. This heap of probable inducements is not of power as a mathematical and physical demonstration, which is in discourse as the sun is in heaven, but it makes a milky and a white path, visible enough to walk securely.

NATURAL APPETITES.

All our trouble is from within us; and if a dish of lettuce and a clear fountain can cool all my heats, so that I shall have neither thirst nor pride, lust nor revenge, envy nor ambition, I am lodged in the bosom of felicity; and, indeed, no men sleep so soundly as they that lay their head upon Nature's lap. For a single dish, and a clear chalice lifted from the springs, can cure my hunger and thirst: but the meat of Ahasuerus's feast cannot satisfy my ambition and my pride. He, therefore, that hath the fewest desires and the most quiet passions, whose wants are soon provided for, and whose possessions

Sermons: "The House of Feasting," part i.

cannot be disturbed with violent fears, he that dwells next door to satisfaction, and can carry his needs and lay them down where he please—this man is the happy man; and this is not to be done in great designs, and swelling fortunes. For as it is in plants which Nature thrusts forth from her navel, she makes regular provisions, and dresses them with strength and ornament, with easiness and full stature; but if you thrust a jessamine there where she would have had a daisy grow, or bring the tall fir from dwelling in his own country, and transport the orange or the almond-tree near the fringes of the north star, Nature is displeased, and becomes unnatural, and starves her sucklings, and renders you a return less than your charge and expectation.

ATHEISM.

Who in the world is a verier fool, a more ignorant, wretched person, than he that is an atheist? A man may better believe there is no such man as himself, and that he is not in being, than that there is no God: for himself can cease to be, and once was not, and shall be changed from what he is, and in very many

Sermons:
"Apples of Sodom,"
part ii.

periods of his life knows not that he is ; and so it is every night with him when he sleeps : but none of these can happen to God ; and if he knows it not, he is a fool. Can anything in this world be more foolish than to think that all this rare fabric of heaven and earth can come by chance, when all the skill of art is not able to make an oyster ? To see rare effects, and no cause; an excellent government and no prince ; a motion without an immovable ; a circle without a centre ; a time without eternity ; a second without a first ; a thing that begins not from itself, and therefore not to perceive there is something from whence it does begin, which must be without beginning ; these things are so against philosophy and natural reason, that he must needs be a beast in his understanding that does not assent to them ; this is the atheist: "The fool hath said in his heart, There is no God." That is his character : the thing framed, says that nothing framed it ; the tongue never made itself to speak, and yet talks against him that did ; saying, that which is made, is, and that which made it, is not.

The Bible.

The Holy Ghost is certainly the best preacher in the world, and the words of Scripture the best sermons.   *"Holy Living," c. iv. sec. 4.*

* * *

Read not much at a time; but meditate as much as your time, and capacity, and disposition will give you leave, ever remembering that little reading and much thinking, little speaking and much hearing, frequent and short prayers, and great devotion, is the best way to be wise, to be holy, to be devout.   *"Golden Grove," Agenda xxiii.*

* * *

In all Scripture there is a spiritual sense, a spiritual cabala, which, as it tends directly to holiness, so it is best and truest understood by the sons of the Spirit, who love God, and therefore know Him.   *Sermons "Preached to the University of Dublin."*

* * *

In all the interpretations of Scripture, the literal sense is to be presumed and chosen, unless there be evident cause to the contrary. The reasons are plain; because the literal sense is natural, and it is first, and it is most agreeable to some things in their whole kind;   *Sermons: "The Whole Duty of the Clergy."*

not indeed to prophecies, nor to the teachings of the learned, nor those cryptic ways of institution by which the ancients did hide a light, and keep it in a dark lantern from the temeration of ruder handlings and popular preachers: but the literal sense is agreeable to laws, to the publication of commands, to the revelation of the Divine will, to the concerns of the vulgar, to the foundations of faith, and to all the notice of things, in which the idiot is as much concerned as the greatest clerks.

BAPTISM.

Baptism is not to be estimated as one act, transient and effective to single purposes; but it is an entrance to a conjugation and a state of blessings.

<small>"The Great Exemplar," part i. sec. ix.</small>

* *

It is not the good lute, but the skilful hand that makes the music; it is not the body, but the soul that is the man; and yet he is not the man without both. For baptism is but the material part in the sacrament; it is the Spirit that giveth life, whose work is faith and repentance, begun by Himself without the sacrament, and con-

<small>Ibid.</small>

signed in the sacrament, and actuated and increased in the co-operation of our whole life.

※ ※

In baptism we are admitted to the kingdom of Christ, presented unto Him, consigned with His sacrament, enter into His militia, give up our understandings and our choice *Ibid.* to the obedience of Christ, and in all senses, that we can, become His disciples, witnessing a good confession and undertaking a holy life. The next step beyond this is adoption into the covenant, which is an immediate consequent of the first presentation; this being the first act of man, that the first act of God. And this is called by St. Paul a being "baptised in one spirit into one body"— that is, we are made capable of the communion of saints, the blessings of the faithful, the privileges of the Church. And therefore baptism is a new birth, by which we enter into the new world, the new creation, the blessings and spiritualities of the kingdom. And this is the expression which our Saviour Himself used to Nicodemus: "Unless a man be born of water and the Spirit." For now we begin to be reckoned in a new census or account; God is become our Father, Christ our Elder Brother, the Spirit the earnest of our inheritance, the Church our Mother; our food is the body and blood of our Lord, faith is our learning, religion our employment, and our whole life is spiritual, and heaven the object of our hopes, and the mighty prize of our high calling.

※ ※

Baptism is the beginning of the new life and an admission of us into the evangelical covenant; which on our parts consists in a sincere and timely endeavour to glorify God by faith and obedience; and on God's part He will pardon what is past, assist us for the future, and not measure us by grains and scruples, or exact our duties by the measure of an angel, but by the span of a man's hand.

<small>Ibid.</small>

CHARITY.

If we cannot labour, yet let us love. Nothing can hinder us from that but our own uncharitableness.

<small>"Holy Dying," c. iv. sec. 2.</small>

※ ※

Charity itself, which is the vertical top of all

religion, is nothing else but a union of joys, concentred in the heart, and reflected from all the angles of our life and intercourse. It is a rejoicing in God, a gladness in our neighbour's good, a pleasure in doing good, a rejoicing with him; and without love we cannot have any joy at all. It is this that makes children to be a pleasure, and friendship to be so noble and divine a thing; and upon this account it is certain that all that which can innocently make a man cheerful, does also make him charitable; for grief, and age, and sickness, and weariness, these are peevish and troublesome; but mirth and cheerfulness are content, and civil, and compliant, and communicative, and love to do good, and swell up to felicity only upon the wings of charity.

Sermons: "The Good and Evil Tongue," part ii.

* * *

I end with a story which I find in the Jews' books:—When Abraham sat at his tent door, according to his custom, waiting to entertain strangers, he espied an old man stooping and leaning on his staff, weary with age and travel, coming towards him, who was a hundred years of age. He received him kindly,

"Liberty of Prophesying," sec. xxii.

washed his feet, provided supper, and caused him to sit down; but observing that the old man eat and prayed not, nor begged for a blessing on his meat, he asked him why he did not worship the God of heaven? The old man told him that he worshipped fire only, and acknowledged no other God: at which answer Abraham grew so zealously angry that he thrust the old man out of his tent and exposed him to all the evils of the night and an unguarded condition. When the old man was gone, God called to Abraham, and asked him where the stranger was. He replied, "I thrust him away because he did not worship Thee." God answered him, "I have suffered him these hundred years, although he dishonoured Me; and couldst thou not endure him one night, when he gave thee no trouble?" Upon this, saith the story, Abraham fetched him back again, and gave him hospitable entertainment and wise instruction: "Go thou and do likewise," and thy charity will be rewarded by the God of Abraham.[1]

[1] The story is to be found in the Bostan of the Persian poet Saadi, but it is quoted in the dedication of a Jewish work, translated by Gentius and published in 1651. The fact that the epilogue did not appear until the publication of the second edition of "The Liberty of Prophesying" makes it the more probable that Taylor

CHRIST OUR EXAMPLE.

He entered into the world with all the circumstances of poverty. He had a star to illustrate His birth; but a stable for His bed-chamber, and a manger for His cradle. The angels sang hymns when He was born; but He was cold and cried, uneasy and unprovided. He lived long in the trade of a carpenter; He, by whom God made the world, had, in His first years, the business of a mean and ignoble trade. He did good wherever He went; and almost wherever He went was abused. He deserved heaven for His obedience, but found a cross in His way thither: and if ever any man had reason to expect fair usages from God, and to be dandled in the lap of ease, softness, and a prosperous fortune, He it was only that could deserve that, or anything that can be good. But after He had chosen to live a life of virtue, of poverty, and labour, He entered into a state of death, whose shame and trouble were great enough to pay for the sins of the whole world.

Sermons: "Faith and Patience of the Saints," part i.

borrowed it from this source. It has been published in several editions of Benjamin Franklin's works as though he were the author, but there is no proof that he claimed it for his own.—ED.

CHRIST A SUFFERER.

All that Christ came for was, or was mingled with, sufferings: for all those little joys which God sent, either to recreate His person, or to illustrate His office, were abated or attended with afflictions; God being more careful to establish in Him the covenant of sufferings than to refresh His sorrows. Presently after the angels had finished their hallelujahs, He was forced to fly to save His life; and the air became full of shrieks of the desolate mothers of Bethlehem for their dying babes. God had no sooner made Him illustrious with a voice from heaven, and the descent of the Holy Ghost upon Him in the waters of baptism, but He was delivered over to be tempted and assaulted by the devil in the wilderness. His transfiguration was a bright ray of glory; but then also He entered into a cloud, and was told a sad story what He was to suffer at Jerusalem. And upon Palm Sunday, when He rode triumphantly into Jerusalem, and was adorned with the acclamations of a King and a God, He wet the palms with His tears, sweeter than the drops of manna, or the little pearls of heaven that

Ibid.

descended upon Mount Hermon; weeping in the midst of this triumph over obstinate, perishing, and malicious Jerusalem. For this Jesus was like the rainbow which God set in the clouds as a sacrament to confirm a promise and establish a grace; He was half made of the glories of the light, and half of the moisture of a cloud; in His best days He was but half triumph and half sorrow: He was sent to tell of His Father's mercies, and that God intended to spare us; but appeared not but in the company or in the retinue of a shower, and of foul weather. But I need not tell that Jesus, beloved of God, was a suffering person: that which concerns this question most is, that He made for us a covenant of sufferings: His doctrines were such as expressly and by consequent enjoin and suppose sufferings, and a state of affliction; His very promises were sufferings; His beatitudes were sufferings; His rewards and His arguments to invite men to follow Him were only taken from sufferings in this life, and the reward of sufferings hereafter.

There is no state in the Church so serene, no

days so prosperous, in which God does not give to His servants the powers and opportunities of suffering for Him; not only they that die for Christ, but they that live according to His laws, shall find some lives to part with, and many ways to suffer for Christ. To kill and crucify the old man and all his lusts, to mortify a beloved sin, to fight against temptations, to do violence to our bodies, to live chastely, to suffer affronts patiently, to forgive injuries and debts, to renounce all prejudice and interest in religion, and to choose our side for truth's sake (not because it is prosperous, but because it pleases God), to be charitable beyond our power, to reprove our betters with modesty and openness, to displease men rather than God, to be at enmity with the world, that you may preserve friendship with God, to own truth in despite of danger or scorn, to despise shame, to refuse worldly pleasures when they tempt your soul beyond duty or safety, to take pains in the cause of religion, the "labour of love," and the crossing of your anger, peevishness, and morosity: these are the daily sufferings of a Christian, and if we perform them well will have the same reward, and an equal smart.

Ibid.

THE CROSS.

The highway of the cross, which the King of sufferings hath trodden before us, is the way to ease, to a kingdom, and to felicity. <small>"Holy Dying," c. iii. sec. 5.</small>

* * *

If we sum up the commandments of Christ we shall find humility, mortification, self-denial, repentance, renouncing the world, mourning, taking up the cross, dying for Him, patience and poverty, to stand in the chiefest rank of Christian precepts, and in the direct order to heaven: "He that will be my disciple must deny himself, and take up his cross and follow Me." We must follow Him that was crowned with thorns and sorrows, Him that was drenched in Cedron, nailed upon the cross, that deserved all good and suffered all evil: that is the sum of Christian religion, as it distinguishes from all religions in the world. <small>Sermons: "Faith and Patience of the Saints," part i.</small>

* * *

Our Lord Jesus certainly intends to admit none to His resurrection but by the doors of His grave, none to glory but by the way of the cross. "If we be planted into the <small>Ibid.</small>

likeness of His death, we shall be also of His resurrection;" else on no terms. Christ took away sin from us, but He left us our share of sufferings; and the cross, which was first printed upon us in the waters of baptism, must for ever be borne by us in penance, in mortification, in self-denial, and in martyrdom and toleration, according as God shall require of us by the changes of the world and the condition of the Church.

CHILDREN.

No man can tell, but he that loves his children, how many delicious accents make a man's heart dance in the pretty conversation of those dear pledges; their childishness, their stammering, their little angers, their innocence, their imperfections, their necessities, are so many little emanations of joy and comfort to him that delights in their persons and society; but he that loves not his wife and children, feeds a lioness at home, and broods a nest of sorrows; and blessing itself cannot make him happy; so that all the commandments of God enjoining a man to "love his wife" are nothing but so many necessities and capacities of joy.

Sermons: "The Marriage Ring," part ii.

Holy Communion.

The holy communion, or supper of the Lord, is not easy to be understood; it is not lightly to be received; it is not much opened in the writings of the New Testament, but still left in its mysterious nature; it is too much untwisted and nicely handled by the writings of the doctors, and by them made more mysterious, and, like a doctrine of philosophy, made intricate by explications, and difficult by the aperture and dissolution of distinctions. So we sometimes espy a bright cloud formed into an irregular figure; when it is observed by unskilful and fantastic travellers, it looks like a centaur to some, and as a castle to others; some tell that they saw an army with banners, and it signifies war; but another, wiser than his fellow, says it looks for all the world like a flock of sheep, and foretells plenty; and all the while it is nothing but a shining cloud, by its own mobility and the activity of a wind cast into a contingent and inartificial shape. So it is in this great mystery of our religion, in which some espy strange things which God intended not, and others see not what God hath plainly told: some call that part of it a mystery

"The Worthy Communicant," Introduction.

which is none, and others think all of it nothing but a mere ceremony and a sign; some say it signifies, and some say it effects; some say it is a sacrifice, and others call it a sacrament; some schools of learning make it the instrument of grace in the hand of God; others say that it is God Himself in that instrument of grace; some call it venerable, and others say, as the vain men in the prophet, that "the table of the Lord is contemptible"; some come to it with their sins on their head, and others with their sins in their mouth; some come to be cured, some to be quickened; some to be nourished, and others to be made alive; some, out of fear and reverence, take it but seldom; others, out of devotion, take it frequently; some receive it as a means to procure great graces and blessings, others as an eucharist, and an office of thanksgiving for what they have received; some call it an act of obedience merely, others account it an excellent devotion, and the exercising of the virtue of religion; some take it to strengthen their faith, others to beget it, and yet many affirm that it does neither, but supposes faith beforehand as a disposition—faith in all its degrees, according to the degree of grace whither the communicant is arrived; some affirm the elements are to be blessed by prayers of the bishop or other minister; others say it is only by the mystical words, the words of institution; and when it is blessed, some believe it to be the natural body of Christ; others to be nothing of that, but the blessings of Christ, His word and His Spirit, His passion in representment, and His grace in real exhibition; and all these men have something of reason for what they pretend; and yet the words of Scripture from whence they pretend are not so many as are the several pretensions.

My purpose is not to dispute, but to persuade; not to confute any one, but to instruct those that need; not to make a noise, but to excite devotion; not to enter into curious, but material inquiries, and to gather together into a union all those several portions of truth, and differing apprehensions of mysteriousness, and various methods and rules of preparation, and seemingly opposed doctrines, by which even good men stand at a distance and are afraid of each other.

We must bring faith along with us, and God will

increase our faith; we must come with charity, and we shall go away with more; we must come with truly penitential hearts; and to him that hath shall be given, and he shall have more abundantly.

Ibid., c. i. sec. v.

※ ※

Happy is that soul which comes to these springs of salvation as "the hart to the water-brooks," panting and thirsty, longing and passionate, weary of sin, and hating vanity, and reaching out the heart and hands to Christ.

Ibid., c. ii. sec. ii.

※ ※

Here we do not only hear the words of Christ, but we obey them; we believe with the heart, and we confess with the mouth, and we act with the hand, and incline the head, and bow the knee, and give our heart in sacrifice; here we come to Christ, and Christ comes to us; here we represent the death of Christ as He would have us represent it, and remember Him as He commanded us to remember Him; here we give Him thanks, and here we give Him ourselves; here we defy all the works of darkness, and hither we come to be invested with a robe of light, by being joined to the "Sun of Righteous-

Ibid., c. iii. sec. v.

ness," to live in His eyes, and to walk by His brightness, and to be refreshed with His warmth, and directed by His Spirit, and united to His glories. So that if we can receive Christ's body and drink His blood, out of the sacrament, much more can we do it in the sacrament.—For this is the chief of all the Christian mysteries, and the union of all Christian blessings, and the investiture of all Christian rights, and the exhibition of the charter of all Christian promises, and the exercise of all Christian duties. Here is the exercise of our faith, and act of obedience, and the confirmation of our hope, and the increase of our charity. So that although God be gracious in every dispensation, yet He is bountiful in this; although we serve God in every virtue, yet in the worthy reception of this Divine sacrament there must be a conjugation of virtues, and, therefore, we serve Him more; He always fills our cup, but here it runs over.

※ ※

He hath appointed to His chosen ones "to eat and drink at His table in His kingdom," plainly teaching us that by eating and drinking Christ is meant in this world to live the life of the Spirit, and in the other world

Ibid., c. i. sec. ii.

it is to live the life of glory. Here we feed upon duty, and there we feed upon reward; our wine is here mingled with water and with myrrh; there it is mere and unmixed; but still it is called meat and drink, and still is meant grace and glory, the fruits of the Spirit, and the joy of the Spirit; that is, by Christ we here live a spiritual life, and hereafter we shall live a life eternal.

⁂

All Christian people must come. They indeed that are in the state of sin must not come so, but yet they must come; first they must quit their state of death, and then partake of the bread of life. They that are at enmity with their neighbours must come; that is no excuse for their not coming; only they must not bring their enmity along with them, but leave it, and then come. They that have variety of secular employment must come; only they must leave their secular thoughts and affections behind them, and then come and converse with God. If any man be well grown in grace, he must needs come, because he is excellently disposed to so holy a feast; but he that is but in the infancy of piety

"Holy Living," c. iv. sec. 10.

had need to come, that so he may grow in grace. The strong must come, lest they become weak, and the weak that they may become strong. The sick must come to be cured, the healthful to be preserved. They that have leisure must come, because they have no excuse; they that have no leisure must come hither, that by so excellent an act of religion they may sanctify their business. The penitent sinners must come that they may be justified, and they that are justified that they may be justified still. They that have fears and great reverence to these mysteries, and think no preparation to be sufficient, must receive, that they may learn how to receive the more worthily ; and they that have a less degree of reverence must come often to have it heightened, that, as those creatures that live amongst the snows of the mountains turn white with their food and conversation with such perpetual whitenesses, so our souls may be transformed into the similitude and union with Christ by our perpetual feeding on Him, and conversation, not only in His courts, but in His very heart and most secret affections and incomparable purities.

CONSCIENCE.

In some cases conscience is like an eloquent and a fair-spoken judge, which declaims not against the criminal, but condemns him justly; in others the judge is more angry, and affrights the prisoner more, but the event is the same. For in those sins where the conscience affrights, and in those in which she affrights not, supposing the sins equal but of differing natures, there is no other difference, but that conscience is a clock, which in one man strikes aloud and gives warning, and in another the hand points silently to the figure, but strikes not; but by this he may as surely see what the other hears, viz., that his hours pass away, and death hastens, and after death comes judgment.

"Ductor Dubitantium," book i. c. i.

CONTENTMENT.

No man is poor that does not think himself so; but if, in a full fortune, with impatience he desires more, he proclaims his wants and his beggarly condition.

"Holy Living," c. ii. sec. 6.

* * *

Is that beast better that hath two or three

mountains to graze on than a little bee that feeds on dew or manna, and lives upon what falls every morning from the storehouses of heaven, clouds and providence? Can a man quench his thirst better out of a river than a full urn, or drink better from the fountain which is finely paved with marble than when it swells over the green turf?

Ibid.

* *

Is not all the world God's family? Are not we His creatures? Are we not as clay in the hand of the potter? Do we not live upon His meat, and move by His strength, and do our work by His light? Are we anything but what we are from Him? And shall there be a mutiny among the flocks and herds because their lord or their shepherd chooses their pastures and suffers them not to wander into deserts and unknown ways? If we choose, we do it so foolishly that we cannot like it long, and most commonly not at all; but God, who can do what He pleases, is wise to choose safely for us, affectionate to comply with our needs, and powerful to execute all His wise decrees. Here, therefore, is the wisdom of the contented man, to let God choose

Ibid.

for him; for when we have given up our wills to Him, and stand in that station of the battle where our great general hath placed us, our spirits must needs rest, while our conditions have, for their security, the power, the wisdom, and the charity of God.

※ ※ ※

Enjoy the blessings of this day, if God send them, and the evils of it bear patiently and sweetly; for this day is only ours; we are dead to yesterday, and we are not yet born to the morrow. He, therefore, that enjoys the present, if it be good, enjoys as much as is possible, and if only that day's trouble leans upon him, it is singular and finite. "Sufficient to the day," said Christ, "is the evil thereof"—sufficient, but not intolerable.

Ibid.

※ ※ ※

The Lord of men and angels was also the King of sufferings: and if thy coarse robe trouble thee, remember the swaddling-clothes of Jesus; if thy bed be uneasy, yet it is not worse than His manger; and it is no sadness to have a thin table if thou callest to mind that

Ibid.

the King of heaven and earth was fed with a little breast-milk, and yet, besides this, He suffered all the sorrows which we deserved. We therefore have great reason to sit down upon our own hearths, and warm ourselves at our own fires, and feed upon content at home; for it were a strange pride to expect to be more gently treated by the Divine Providence than the best and wisest men, than apostles and saints, nay, the Son of the eternal God, the heir of both the worlds.

A Threefold Cord.

Faith believes the revelations of God; hope expects His promises; and charity loves His excellencies and mercies. Faith gives us understanding to God; hope gives *"Holy Living," c. iv.* up all the passions and affections to heaven and heavenly things; and charity gives the will to the service of God. Faith is opposed to infidelity, hope to despair, charity to enmity and hostility; and these three sanctify the whole man, and make our duty to God and obedience to His commandments to be chosen, reasonable, and delightful, and therefore to be entire, persevering, and universal.

COVETOUSNESS.

"Holy Living,"
c. iv. sec. 8.

No wealth can satisfy the covetous desire of wealth.

DESPAIR.

It is impossible for that man to despair who remembers that his helper is omnipotent, and can do what He pleases. Let us rest there awhile: He can, if He please; and He is infinitely loving, willing enough; and He is infinitely wise, choosing better for us than we can do for ourselves. This, in all ages and chances, hath supported the afflicted people of God, and carried them on dry ground through a Red Sea.

Ibid.,
c. iv. sec. 2.

DEATH.

Every day's necessity calls for a reparation of that portion which death fed on all night, when we lay in his lap and slept in his outer chambers. The very spirits of a man prey upon the daily portion of bread and flesh, and every meal is a rescue from one death and lays up for another; and while we think a thought we die; and the clock strikes and reckons on our

"Holy Dying,"
c. i. sec. 1.

portion of eternity; we form our words with the breath of our nostrils, we have the less to live upon for every word we speak. Nature hath given us one harvest every year, but death hath two; and the spring and the autumn send throngs of men and women to charnel-houses; and all the summer long men are recovering from their evils of the spring till the dog-days come, and then the Sirian star makes the summer deadly; and the fruits of autumn are laid up for all the year's provision, and the man that gathers them eats and surfeits, and dies and needs them not, and himself is laid up for eternity; and he that escapes till winter only stays for another opportunity, which the distempers of that quarter minister to him with great variety. Thus death reigns in all the portions of our time. The autumn with its fruits provides disorders for us, and the winter's cold turns them into sharp diseases, and the spring brings flowers to strew our hearse, and the summer gives green turf and brambles to bind upon our graves. Calentures and surfeit, cold and agues, are the four quarters of the year, and all minister to death; and you can go no whither, but you tread upon a dead man's bones.

It is a thing that every one suffers, even persons of the lowest resolution, of the meanest virtue, of no breeding, of no discourse. Take away but the pomps of death, the disguises and solemn bugbears, the tinsel, and the actings by candle-light, and proper and fantastic ceremonies, the minstrels and the noise-makers, the women and the weepers, the swoonings and the shriekings, the nurses and the physicians, the dark room and the ministers, the kindred and the watches; and then to die is easy, ready, and quitted from its troublesome circumstances. It is the same harmless thing that a poor shepherd suffered yesterday, or a maid-servant to-day; and at the same time in which you die, in that very night a thousand creatures die with you, some wise men, and many fools; and the wisdom of the first will not quit him, and the folly of the latter does not make him unable to die.

Ibid. c. iii. sec. 7.

* *

To die is necessary and natural, and it may be honourable; but to die poorly and basely and sinfully, that alone is it that can make a man unfortunate. No man can be a slave but he that fears pain or fears to die.

"Holy Living," c. ii. sec. 6.

Death meets us everywhere, and is procured by every instrument and in all chances, and enters in at many doors: by violence and secret influence; by the aspect of a star and the stink of a mist; by the emissions of a cloud and the meeting of a vapour; by the fall of a chariot and the stumbling at a stone; by a full meal or an empty stomach; by watching at the wine or by watching at prayers; by the sun or the moon; by a heat or a cold; by sleepless nights or sleeping days; by water frozen into the hardness and sharpness of a dagger, or water thawed into the floods of a river; by a hair or a raisin; by violent motion or sitting still; by severity or dissolution; by God's mercy or God's anger; by everything in providence and everything in manners; by everything in nature and everything in chance.

<small>"Holy Dying," c. i. sec. 1.</small>

It is a mighty change that is made by the death of every person, and it is visible to us who are alive. Reckon but from the sprightfulness of youth, and the fair cheeks and full eyes of childhood, from the vigorousness and strong flexure of the joints of five-and-twenty

<small>Ibid. c. i. sec. 2.</small>

to the hollowness and dead paleness, to the loathsomeness and horror of a three days' burial, and we shall perceive the distance to be very great and very strange. But so have I seen a rose newly springing from the clefts of its hood, and at first it was fair as the morning, and full with the dew of heaven, as a lamb's fleece; but when a ruder breath had forced open its virgin modesty, and dismantled its too youthful and unripe retirements, it began to put on darkness, and to decline to softness and the symptoms of a sickly age; it bowed the head and broke its stalk, and at night, having lost some of its leaves and all its beauty, it fell into the portion of weeds and outworn faces. The same is the portion of every man and every woman.

* *

I have conversed with some men who rejoiced in the death or calamity of others, and accounted it as a judgment upon them for being on the other side, and against them in the contention; but within the revolution of a few months the same man met with a more uneasy and unhandsome death, which when I saw I wept

Ibid., c. i. sec. 1.

and was afraid, for I knew that it must be so with all men; for we also shall die, and end our quarrels and contentions by passing to a final sentence.

THE FEAR OF DEATH.

The religion of a Christian does more command fortitude than ever did any institution; for we are commanded to be willing to die for Christ, to die for the brethren, to die rather than to give offence or scandal: the effect of which is this—that he that is instructed to do the necessary parts of his duty is, by the same instrument, fortified against death: as he that does his duty need not fear death, so neither shall he; the parts of his duty are parts of his security. It is certainly a great baseness and pusillanimity of spirit that makes death terrible, and extremely to be avoided.

<small>Ibid. c. iii. sec. 8.</small>

* *

I do not say it is a sin to be afraid of death: we find the boldest spirit, that discourses of it with confidence, and dares undertake a danger as big as death, yet doth shrink at the horror of it when it comes dressed in its proper circumstances. And Brutus, who was

<small>Ibid.</small>

as bold a Roman to undertake a noble action as any was since they first reckoned by consuls, yet when Furius came to cut his throat after his defeat by Anthony he ran from it like a girl, and being admonished to die constantly, he swore by his life that he would shortly endure death. But what do I speak of such imperfect persons? Our blessed Lord was pleased to legitimate fear to us by His agony and prayers in the garden. It is not a sin to be afraid, but it is a great felicity to be without fear; which felicity our dearest Saviour refused to have, because it was agreeable to His purposes to suffer anything that was contrary to felicity, everything but sin.

DUELS.

That which men in this question call honour is nothing but a reputation amongst persons vain, unchristian in their deportment, empty and ignorant souls, who count that the standard of honour which is the instrument of reprobation; as if to be a gentleman were to be no Christian. They that have built their reputation upon such societies must take new estimates of it, according as the wine, or fancy, or custom,

<small>"The Great Exemplar," part ii. sec. 12.</small>

or some great fighting person, shall determine it; and whatsoever invites a quarrel is a rule of honour. But then it is a sad consideration to remember that it is accounted honour not to recede from anything we have said or done: it is honour not to take the lie, in the meantime it is not dishonourable to lie indeed, but to be told so; and not to kill him that says it, and venture my life and his too, that is a forfeiture of reputation. A mistress's favour, an idle discourse, a jest, a jealousy, a health, a gaiety, anything must engage two lives in hazard, and two souls in ruin—or else they are dishonoured. As if a life, which is so dear to a man's self, which ought to be dear to others, which all laws and wise princes and states have secured by the circumvallation of laws and penalties, which nothing but Heaven can recompense for the loss of, which is the breath of God, which to preserve Christ died, the Son of God died; as if this were so contemptible a thing that it must be ventured for satisfaction of a vicious person, or a vain custom, or such a folly which a wise and a severe person had rather die than be guilty of. Honour is from him that honours: now certainly God and the king are the fountains of honour; right reason and religion, the Scripture and the laws, are the best rules of estimating honour; and if we offer to account our honours by the senseless and illiterate discourses of vain and vicious persons, our honour can be no greater than the fountain from whence it is derivative; and at this rate Harpaste, Seneca's wife's fool, might have declared Thersites an honourable person, and every bold gladiator in a Roman theatre, or a fighting rebel among the slaves of Sparta, or a trooper of Spartacus's guard, might have stood upon their honour upon equal and as fair a challenge.

THE LINES OF DUTY.

The counsels of God are not like the oracles of Apollo, double in their sense, intricate in their expression, secret in their meaning, deceitful in their measures, and otherwise in the event than they could be in their expectation. But the word of God, in the lines of duty, is open as the face of heaven, bright as the moon, healthful as the sun's influence; and this is certainly true—that when a thing becomes obscure, though it may oblige us to a prudent search, yet it

;"Ductor Dubitantium," book i. c. vi.

binds us not under a guilt, but only so far as it is or may be plainly understood.

EMPLOYMENT.

Let your employment be such as may become a reasonable person, and not be a business fit for children or distracted people, but fit for your age and understanding. For a *"Holy Living," c. i. sec. 1.* man may be very idly busy, and take great pains to so little purpose, that in his labours and expense of time he shall serve no end but of folly and vanity. There are some trades that wholly serve the ends of idle persons and fools, and such as are fit to be seized upon by the severity of laws and banished from under the sun, and there are some people who are busy, but it is, as Domitian was, in catching flies.

Let your employment be fitted to your person and calling. Some there are that employ their time in affairs infinitely below the dignity of their person, and being called by God or by the republic to help to bear great burdens and to judge a people, do enfeeble their understandings and disable their persons by sordid and brutish business. Thus Nero went up and down Greece, and challenged the fiddlers at their trade. Æropus, a Macedonian king, made lanterns; Harcatius, the king of Parthia, was a mole-catcher; and Biantes, the Lydian, filed needles. He that is appointed to minister in holy things must not suffer secular affairs and sordid arts to eat up great portions of his employment; a clergyman must not keep a tavern, nor a judge be an innkeeper. Such employments are the diseases of labour and the rust of time, which it contracts, not by lying still, but by dirty employment.

Faith.

If you dare trust to God when the case, to human reason, seems impossible, and trust to God then also out of choice, not because you have nothing else to trust to, but because He is the only support of a just confidence, then you give a good testimony of your faith.

<small>Ibid., c. iv. sec. 1.</small>

* *

A little faith, casting its weak beams on Christ and His death, will go far. The quantity of a grain of mustard-seed hath warmth and virtue in it to spread abundantly. If faith on earth hath shaken off all frailty and

<small>"Christian Consolations," c. i.</small>

comprehended the joys of heaven without casting its eye aside to the love of this world, I do not conceive how the body could subsist any longer here, but that the soul, in that ecstasy, would be dissolved and fly away.

* * *

Faith and repentance are the whole duty of a Christian. Faith is a sacrifice of the understanding to God; repentance sacrifices the whole will: that gives the knowing; this gives up all the desiring faculties: that makes us disciples; this makes us servants of the holy Jesus. Nothing else was preached by the Apostles, nothing was enjoined as the duty of man, nothing else did build up the body of Christian religion. So that as faith contains all that knowledge which is necessary to salvation, so repentance comprehends in it all the whole practice and working duty of a returning Christian. *Sermons: "Invalidity of a late or death-bed repentance," part ii.*

* * *

Whatsoever is good, if it be a grace, it is an act of faith; if it be a reward, it is the fruit of faith. So that as all the actions of men are but the productions of the soul, so are all the actions of the new man the effects of faith. *"The Great Exemplar," part ii. sec. 10.*

For faith is the life of Christianity, and a good life is the life of faith.

Faith gives a new light to the soul, but it does not put our eyes out; and what God hath given us in our nature could never be intended as a snare to religion, or to engage us to believe a lie. Faith sees more in the sacrament than the eye does, and tastes more than the tongue does, but nothing against it; and as God hath not two wills contradictory to each other, so neither hath He given us two notices and perceptions of objects, whereof the one is affirmative and the other negative of the same thing.

[side note: "The Worthy Communicant," c. iii. sec. 3.]

Whatsoever is against right reason, that no faith can oblige us to believe; for although reason is not the positive and affirmative measure of our faith, and God can do no more than we can understand, and our faith ought to be larger than our reason, and take something into her heart that reason can never take into her eye—yet in all our creed there can be nothing against reason. If true reason justly contradicts an article, it is not "of the household of faith." In this there is no difficulty, but that in practice we take care that we do not call that reason which is not so; for although a man's reason is a right judge, yet it ought not to pass sentence in an inquiry of faith until all the information be brought in—all that is within, and all that is without; all that is above, and all that is below; all that concerns it in experience, and all that concerns it in act; whatsoever is of pertinent observation, and whatsoever is revealed; for else reason may argue very well, and yet conclude falsely; it may conclude well in logic, and yet infer a false proposition in theology; but when our judge is fully and truly informed in all that where she is to make her judgment, we may safely follow it whithersoever she invites us.

The Principle of Faith.

Some are so ingeniously miserable that they will never believe a proposition in divinity if anything can be said against it; they will be credulous enough in all the affairs of their life, but impenetrable by a sermon of the gospel; they will believe the word of a man and the promise of their neighbour, but a promise of Scripture signifies nothing unless it can be proved like a proposition in the metaphysics. If Sempro-

Ibid., c. iii. sec. 4.

nius tells them a story, it is sufficient if he be a just man, and the narrative be probable; but though religion be taught by many excellent men, who gave their lives for a testimony, this shall not pass for truth till there is no objection left to stand against it. The reason of these things is plain: they do not love the thing; their interest is against it; they have no joy in religion; they are not willing and desirous that the things shall appear true. When love is the principle, the thing is easy to the understanding; the objections are nothing, the arguments are good, and the preachers are in the right. Faith assents to the revelations of the gospel, not only because they are well proved, but because they are excellent things; not only because my reason is convinced, but my reason yields upon the fairer terms because my affections are gained. For if faith were an assent to an article but just so far as it is demonstrated, then faith were no virtue, and infidelity were no sin, because in this there is no choice and no refusal. But where that which is probable is also naturally indemonstrable, and yet the conclusion is that in which we must rejoice, and that for which we must earnestly contend, and that in the belief of which we serve God, and that for which we must be ready to die—it is certain that the understanding observing the credibility, and the will being pleased with the excellency, they produce a zeal of belief because they together make up the demonstration. For a reason can be opposed by a reason, and an argument by an argument; but if I love my religion, nothing can take me from it, unless it can pretend to be more useful and more amiable, more perfective and more excellent, than heaven and immortality, and a kingdom and a crown of peace, and all the things and all the glories of the eternal God.

VAIN FAITH.

The kingdom of God did not, then, consist in words, but in power—the power of godliness—though now we are fallen into another method; we have turned all religion into faith, Sermons: "Fides Formata." and our faith is nothing but the productions of interest or disputing; it is adhering to a party, and a wrangling against all the world beside; and when it is asked of what religion he is of, we understand the meaning to be what faction does he follow, what are the articles of his sect, not what is the manner of his life; and if men be zealous for their party and that interest, then they are precious men, though otherwise they be covetous as the grave, factious as Dathan, schismatical as Korah, or proud as the fallen angels.

TRUE FAITH.

True Christian faith must have in it something of obscurity, something that must be made up <small>"The Worthy Communicant," c. iii. sec. 4.</small> by duty and by obedience; but it is nothing but this—we must trust the evidence of God in the obscurity of the thing. God's testimony must be clear to him, and the thing, in all other senses, not clear; and then to trust the article because God hath said it, it must have in it an excellency which God loves, and that He will reward. In order to this it is highly considerable that the greatest argument to prove our religion is the goodness and the holiness of it; it is that which makes peace and friendships, content and comfort, which unites all relations, and endears the relatives; it relieves the needy and defends the widow; it ends strife, and makes love endless. All other arguments can be opposed and tempted by wit and malice, but against the goodness of the religion no man can speak; by which it appears that the greatest argument is that which moves love, intending, by love, to convince the understanding.

FASTING.

All fasting is to be used with prudence and charity, for there is no end to which fasting serves but may be obtained by other instruments; and therefore it must, at no hand, be made an instrument of scruple or become an enemy to our health, or be imposed upon persons that are sick or aged or to whom it is, in any sense, uncharitable, such as are wearied travellers, or to whom, in the whole kind of it, it is useless, such as are women with child, poor people, and little children. But in these cases the Church hath made provision and inserted caution into her laws; and they are to be reduced to practice, according to custom and the sentence of prudent persons, with great latitude, and without niceness and curiosity, having this in our first care, that we secure our virtue, and next, that we secure our health, that we may the better exercise the labours

"Holy Living," c. iv. sec. 5.

of virtue, lest out of too much austerity we bring ourselves to that condition that it be necessary to be indulgent to softness, ease, and extreme tenderness.

THE FATHERS.

He that says that we may dissent from the fathers, when we have a reason greater than that authority, does no way oppose him that says you ought not to dissent from what they say when you have no reason great enough to outweigh it. He that says the words of the fathers are not sufficient to determine a nice question stands not against him who says they are excellent corroboratives in a question already determined and practised accordingly. He that says the sayings of the fathers are no demonstration in a question may say true, and yet he that says it is a degree of probability may say true, too. He that says they are not our masters speaks consonantly to the words of Christ, but he that denies them to be good instructors does not speak agreeably to reason or to the sense of the Church.

"Episcopacy Asserted," Dedication.

Spiritual Freedom.

Some persons there are who dare not sin; they dare not omit their hours of prayer, and they are restless in their spirits till they have done; but they go to it as to execution; they stay from it as long as they can, and they drive, like Pharoah's chariots, with the wheels off, sadly and heavily; and, besides that, such persons have reserved to themselves the best part of their sacrifice, and do not give their will to God; they do not love Him with all their heart, they are also soonest tempted to retire and fall off. Sextius Romanus resigned the honours and offices of the city and betook himself to the severity of a philosophical life; but when his unusual diet and hard labour began to pinch his flesh and he felt his propositions smart, and that which was fine in discourse at a symposiac or an academical dinner began to sit uneasily upon him in the practice, he so despaired that he had like to have cast himself into the sea to appease the labours of his religion, because he never had gone farther than to think it a fine thing to be a wise man; he would commend it, but he was loath to pay for it at the price that

<small>Sermons: "Of Growth in Grace," part i.</small>

God and the philosopher set upon it. But he that is "grown in grace," and hath made religion habitual to his spirit, is not at ease but when he is doing the works of the new man; he rests in religion, and comforts his sorrows with thinking of his prayers; and in all crosses of the world he is patient, because his joy is at hand to refresh him when he list, for he cares not so he may serve God; and if you make him poor here, he is rich there, and he counts that to be his proper service, his work, his recreation, and reward.

FRIENDSHIP.

Every man rejoices twice when he hath a partner of his joy. A friend shares my sorrow, and makes it but a moiety; but he swells my joy, and makes it double. For so two channels divide the river, and lessen it into rivulets, and make it fordable, and apt to be drunk up at the first revels of the Sirian star; but two torches do not divide, but increase the flame. And though my tears are the sooner dried up when they run upon my friend's cheeks in the furrows of compassion, yet when my flame hath kindled his lamp, we unite the glories, and make them radiant,

Sermons: "The Miracles of the Divine Mercy," part ii.

like the golden candlesticks that burn before the throne of God, because they shine by numbers, by unions, and confederations of light and joy.

Because friendship is that by which the world is most blessed and receives most good, it ought to be chosen amongst the worthiest persons, that is, amongst those that can do greatest benefit to each other; and though in equal worthiness I may choose by my eye, or ear, that is, into the consideration of the essential I may take in also the accidental and extrinsic worthinesses, yet I ought to give every one their just value. When the internal beauties are equal, these shall help to weigh down the scale, and I will love a worthy friend that can delight me as well as profit me rather than him who cannot delight me at all and profit me no more; but yet I will not weigh the gayest flowers or the wings of butterflies against wheat; but when I am to choose wheat I may take that which looks the brightest. I had rather see thyme and roses, marjoram and July flowers, that are fair, sweet, and medicinal, than the prettiest tulips that are good for nothing;

"The Nature, Offices, and Measures of Friendship."

and my sheep and kine are better servants than racehorses and greyhounds, and I shall rather furnish my study with Plutarch and Cicero, with Livy and Polybius, than with Cassandra and Ibrahim Bassa; and if I do give an hour to these for divertisement or pleasure, yet I will dwell with them that can instruct me and make me wise and eloquent, severe and useful to myself and others.

*_**

A man is the best friend in trouble, but a woman may be equal to him in the days of joy; a woman can as well increase our comforts, but cannot so well lessen our sorrows; and therefore we do not carry women with us when we go to fight, but in peaceful cities and times, virtuous women are the beauties of society and the prettinesses of friendship. And when we consider that few persons in the world have all those excellences by which friendship can be useful and illustrious, we may as well allow women as men to be friends; since they can have all that which can be necessary and essential to friendships, and these cannot have all by which friendships can be accidentally improved. In all, some abatements will be made,

Ibid.

and we shall do too much honour to women if we reject them from friendships because they are not perfect; for if to friendships we admit imperfect men because no man is perfect, he that rejects women does find fault with them because they are not more perfect than men, which either does secretly affirm that they ought and can be perfect, or else it openly accuses men of injustice and partiality.

* * *

When you admonish your friend, let it be without bitterness; when you chide him, let it be without reproach; when you praise him, let it be with worthy purposes and for just causes, and in friendly measures; too much of that is flattery, too little is envy; if you do it justly, you teach him true measures; but when others praise him, rejoice, though they praise not thee, and remember that if thou esteemest his praise to be thy disparagement thou art envious, but neither just nor kind.

Ibid.

When all things else are equal, prefer an old friend before a new. If thou meanest to spend thy friend, and make a gain of him till he be weary, thou wilt esteem him as a beast of burden, the worse for his age ; but if thou esteemest him by noble measures, he will be better to thee by thy being used to him, by trial and experience, by reciprocation of endearments, and an habitual worthiness. An old friend is like old wine, which, when a man hath drunk, he doth not desire new, because he saith the old is better. But every old friend was new once ; and if he be worthy, keep the new one till he become old.

THE LIMITATIONS OF FRIENDSHIP.

I pray for all mankind, I am grieved at every sad story I hear ; I am troubled when I hear of a pretty bride murdered in her bride-chamber by an ambitious and enraged rival ; I shed a tear when I am told that a brave king was misunderstood, then slandered, then imprisoned, and then put to death by evil men ; and I can never read the story of the Parisian massacre, or the Sicilian vespers, but my blood curdles and I am disordered by two or three affections. A good man is a friend to all the world ; and he is not truly charitable that does not wish well, and do good to all mankind in what he can.

Ibid.

The effect of this consideration is, that the universal friendship of which I speak must be limited, because we are so. In those things where we stand next to immensity and infinity, as in good wishes and prayers and a readiness to benefit all mankind, in these our friendships must not be limited; but in other things which pass under our hand and eye, our voices and our material exchanges, our hands can reach no farther but to our arms' end, and our voices can but sound till the next air be quiet, and therefore they can have intercourse but within the sphere of their own activity; our needs and our conversations are served by a few, and they cannot reach to all; where they can they must, but where it is impossible it cannot be necessary. It must therefore follow that our friendships to mankind may admit variety as does our conversation; and as by nature we are made sociable to all, so we are friendly; but as all cannot actually be of our society, so neither can all be admitted to a special, actual friendship.

Fear of God.

Fear is the duty we owe to God, as being the God of power and justice, the great Judge of heaven and earth, the avenger of the cause of widows, the patron of the poor, and the advocate of the oppressed, a mighty God and terrible, and so essential an enemy to sin that He spared not His own Son, but gave Him over to death, and to become a sacrifice, when He took upon Him our nature, and became a person obliged for our guilt. Fear is the great bridle of intemperance, the modesty of the spirit, and the restraint of gaieties and dissolutions; it is the girdle to the soul, and the handmaid to repentance, the arrest of sin, and the cure or antidote to the spirit of reprobation; it preserves our apprehensions of the Divine Majesty, and hinders our single actions from combining to sinful habits; it is the mother of consideration and the nurse of sober counsels; and it puts the soul to fermentation and activity, making it to pass from trembling to caution, from caution to carefulness, from carefulness to watchfulness, from thence to prudence; and, by the gates and pro-

Sermons: "Of Godly Fear," part iii.

gresses of repentance, it leads the soul on to love, and to felicity, and to joys in God that shall never cease again. Fear is the guard of a man in the day's prosperity, and it stands upon the watch-towers, and spies the approaching danger, and gives warning to them that laugh loud and feast in the chambers of rejoicing, where a man cannot consider by reason of the noises of wine and jest and music; and if prudence takes it by the hand and leads it on to duty, it is a state of grace, and a universal instrument to infant religion, and the only security of the less perfect persons; and in all senses, is that homage we owe to God, who sends often to demand it, even then when He speaks in thunder, or smites by a plague, or awakens us by threatenings, or discomposes our easiness by sad thoughts, and tender eyes, and fearful hearts, and trembling considerations.

If we fear God as an enemy—an enemy of our sins, and of our persons for their sakes—as yet this fear is but a servile fear; it cannot be a filial fear, since we ourselves *Ibid. part ii.* are not sons; but if this servile fear makes us to desire to be reconciled to God, that He may no longer stay at enmity with us, from this fear we shall soon pass to carefulness, from carefulness to love, from love to diligence, from diligence to perfection; and the enemies shall become servants, and the servants shall become adopted sons, and pass into the society and the participation of the inheritance of Jesus: for this fear is also reverence, and then our God, instead of being "a consuming fire," shall become to us the circle of a glorious crown, and a globe of eternal light.

Vain Fear.

Fear, when it is inordinate, is never a good counsellor, nor makes a good friend; and he that fears God as his enemy is the most completely miserable person in the world. For if he with reason believes God to be his enemy, then the man needs no other argument to prove that he is undone than this, that the fountain of blessing (in this state in which the man is) will never issue anything upon him but cursings. But if he fears this without reason, he makes his fears true by the very suspicion of God, doing Him dishonour, and

Ibid., part iii.

then doing those fond and trifling acts of jealousy which will make God to be what the man feared he already was. We do not know God if we can think any hard thing concerning Him. If God be merciful, let us only fear to offend Him; but then let us never be fearful that He will destroy us, when we are careful not to displease Him. There are some persons so miserable and scrupulous, such perpetual tormentors of themselves with unnecessary fears, that their meat and drink is a snare to their consciences; if they eat, they fear they are gluttons; if they fast, they fear they are hypocrites; and if they would watch, they complain of sleep as of a deadly sin; and every temptation, though resisted, makes them cry for pardon; and every return of such an accident makes them think God is angry; and every anger of God will break them in pieces.

These persons do not believe noble things concerning God; they do not think that He is as ready to pardon them as they are to pardon a sinning servant; they do not believe how much God delights in mercy, nor how wise He is to consider and to make abatement for our unavoidable infirmities; they make judgment of themselves by the measures of an angel, and take the account of God by the proportions of a tyrant. The best that can be said concerning such persons is, that they are hugely tempted or hugely ignorant.

* * *

I have often seen young and unskilful persons sitting in a little boat, when every little wave sporting about the sides of the vessel and every motion and dancing of the barge seemed a danger, and made them cling fast upon their fellows; and yet all the while they were as safe as if they sat under a tree, while a gentle wind shook the leaves into a refreshment and a cooling shade: and the unskilful, inexperienced Christian shrieks out whenever his vessel shakes, thinking it always a danger that the watery pavement is not stable and resident like a rock, and yet all his danger is in himself, none at all from without: for he is indeed moving upon the waters, but fastened to a rock; faith is his foundation, and hope is his anchor, and death is his harbour, and Christ is his pilot, and heaven is his country, and all the evils of poverty or affronts of tribunals and evil

<small>Sermons: "Faith and Patience of the Saints," part iii.</small>

judges, of fears and sadder apprehensions, are but like a loud wind blowing from the right point, they make a noise, and drive faster to the harbour; and if we do not leave the ship and leap into the sea, quit the interests of religion, and run to the securities of the world, cut our cables and dissolve our hopes, grow impatient and hug a wave and die in its embraces, we are as safe at sea, safer in the storm which God sends us, than in a calm when we are befriended with the world.

FUNERALS.

Something is to be given to custom, something to fame, to nature, and to civilities, and to the honour of the deceased friends; for that man is esteemed to die miserable *"Holy Dying," c. v. sec. 8.* for whom no friend or relative sheds a tear, or pays a solemn sigh. I desire to die a *dry death*, but am not very desirous to have a *dry funeral;* some flowers sprinkled upon my grave would do well and comely, and a soft shower to turn those flowers into a springing memory or a fair rehearsal, that I may not go forth of my doors as my servants carry the entrails of beasts.

The Rewards of Godliness.

The godly man is timorous, and yet safe; tossed by the seas, and yet safe at anchor; impaired by evil accidents, and righted by Divine comforts; made sad with a black cloud, and refreshed with a more gentle influence; abused by the world, and yet an heir of heaven; hated by men, and beloved by God; he loses one house, and gets a hundred; he quits a convenient lodging-room, and purchases a glorious country; is forsaken by his friends, but never by a good conscience; he fares hardly, and sleeps sweetly; he flies from his enemies, but hath no distracting fears; he is full of thought, but of no amazement; it is his business to be troubled, and his portion to be comforted; he hath nothing to afflict him, but the loss of that which might be his danger, but can never be his good; and in the recompense of this he hath God for his father, Christ for his captain, the Holy Ghost for his supporter; so that he shall have all the good which God can give him, and of all that good he hath the Holy Trinity for an earnest and a gage for his maintenance at the present, and his portion to all eternity.

Sermons: "Faith and Patience of the Saints," part iii.

Good out of Evil.

When the north wind blows hard, and it rains sadly, none but fools sit down in it and cry; wise people defend themselves against it with a warm garment, or a good fire and a dry roof. *"Holy Living," c. ii. sec. 6.* When a storm of a sad mischance beats upon our spirits, turn it into some advantage by observing where it can serve another end, either of religion or prudence, or more safety or less envy: it will turn into something that is good if we list to make it so; at least it may make us weary of the world's vanity, and take off our confidence from uncertain riches, and make our spirits to dwell in those regions where content dwells essentially. If it does any good to our souls, it hath made more than sufficient recompense for all the temporal affliction. He that threw a stone at a dog and hit his cruel step-mother, said that although he intended it otherwise yet the stone was not quite lost; and if we fail in the first design, if we bring it home to another equally to content us, or more to profit us, then we have put our conditions past the power of chance.

✳ ✳

The greatest evils are from within us, and from ourselves also we must look for our greatest good: for God is the fountain of it, but reaches it to us by our own hands; and when all things look sadly round about us, then only we shall find how excellent a fortune it is to have God to our friend, and of all friendships, that only is created to support us in our needs.

<small>Ibid.</small>

* * *

The question is, whether all this may not, or be not intended to, bring good to us? Not whether God smiles or no, but to what purpose He smiles? not whether this be not evil, but whether this evil will not bring good to us? If we do believe, why are we without comfort and without patience? If we do not believe it, where is our faith?

<small>"The Worthy Communicant," c. iii. sec. 4.</small>

God's Grace.

Christ freely died for us, God pardons us freely in our first access to Him; we could never deserve pardon, because when we need pardon we are enemies, and have no good thing in us; and He freely gives us of His Spirit, and freely He enables us to obey Him; and for

<small>Sermons: "Fides Formata."</small>

our little imperfect services He freely and bountifully will give us eternal life; here is free grace all the way, and he overvalues his pitiful services, who thinks that he deserves heaven by them; and that if he does his duty tolerably, eternal life is not a free gift to him, but a deserved reward.

※ ※

The man that designs his son for noble employments, to honours and to triumphs, to consular dignities and presidencies of councils, loves to see him pale with study, or panting with labour, hardened with sufferance, or eminent by dangers. And so God dresses us for heaven. He loves to see us struggling with a disease, and resisting the devil, and contesting against the weaknesses of nature, and against hope to believe in hope; resigning ourselves to God's will, praying Him to choose for us, and dying in all things but faith and its blessed consequences; *ut ad officium cum periculo simus prompti:* and the danger and the resistance shall endear the office. For so have I known the boisterous north wind pass through the yielding air, which opened its bosom and appeased its violence by entertaining it with easy compliance in all the regions of its

"Holy Dying,"
c. iii. sec. 6.

reception: but when the same breath of heaven hath been checked with the stiffness of a tower, or the united strength of a wood, it grew mighty and dwelt there, and made the highest branches stoop, and make a smooth path for it on the top of all its glories. So is sickness, and so is the grace of God: when sickness hath made the difficulty, then God's grace hath made a triumph, and by doubling its power hath created new proportions of a reward; and then shows its biggest glory when it hath the greatest difficulty to master, the greatest weaknesses to support, the most busy temptations to contest with; for so God loves that His strength should be seen in our weakness and our danger.

God's Providence.

Does not God provide for all the birds, and beasts, and fishes? Do not the sparrows fly from their bush, and every morning find meat where they laid it not? Do not the young ravens call to God, and He feeds them? And were it reasonable that the sons of the family should fear the Father would give meat to the chickens and the servants, his sheep and his dogs, but give none to them? He were a very ill father

<small>"Holy Living," c. ii. sec. 6.</small>

that should do so; or he were a very foolish son that should think so of a good father. But, besides the reasonableness of this faith and this hope, we have infinite experience of it. How innocent, how careless, how secure, is infancy! and yet how certainly provided for! We have lived at God's charges all the days of our life, and have (as the Italian proverb says) set down to meat at the sound of a bell; and hitherto He hath not failed us: we have no reason to suspect Him for the future. We do not use to serve men so; and less time of trial creates great confidences in us towards them, who for twenty years together never broke their word with us; and God hath so ordered it, that a man shall have had the experience of many years' provision before he shall understand how to doubt; that he may be provided for an answer against the temptation shall come, and the mercies felt in his childhood may make him fearless when he is a man. Add to this, that God hath given us His Holy Spirit; He hath promised heaven to us; He hath given us His Son; and we are taught from Scripture to make this inference from hence, "How should not He with Him give us all things else?"

Some men are highly tempted, and are brought to a strait, that, without a miracle, they cannot be relieved; what shall they do? It may be their pride or vanity hath brought the necessity upon them, and it is not a need of God's making; and if it be not they must cure it themselves by lessening their desires and moderating their appetites. And yet, if it be innocent, though unnecessary, God does usually relieve such necessities; and He does not only upon our prayers grant us more than He promised of temporal things, but also He gives many times more than we ask. This is no object for our faith, but ground enough for a temporal and prudent hope; and, if we fail in the particular, God will turn it to a bigger mercy, if we submit to His dispensation, and adore Him in the denial. But if it be a matter of necessity, let not any man, by way of impatience, cry out that God will not work a miracle; for God, by miracle, did give meat and drink to His people in the wilderness, of which He had made no particular promise in any covenant; and if all natural means fail, it is certain that God will rather work a miracle than break His word: He can do that; He cannot do

Ibid.

this. Only we must remember that our portion of temporal things is but food and raiment. God hath not promised us coaches and horses, rich houses and jewels, Tyrian silks and Persian carpets; neither hath He promised to minister to our needs in such circumstances as we shall appoint, but such as Himself shall choose. God will either enable thee to pay thy debt (if thou beggest it of Him), or else He will pay it for thee; that is, take thy desire as a discharge of thy duty, and pay it to thy creditor in blessings, or in some secret of His providence. It may be He hath laid up the corn that shall feed thee in the granary of thy brother, or will clothe thee with his wool. He enabled St. Peter to pay his gabel by the ministry of a fish; and Elias to be waited on by a crow, who was both his minister and his steward for provisions; and His holy Son rode in triumph upon an ass that grazed in another man's pastures. And if God gives to Him the dominion, and reserves the use to thee, thou hast the better half of the two; but the charitable man serves God and serves thy need; and both join to provide for thee, and God blesses both. But if He takes away the flesh-pots from thee He can also alter the appetite, and He hath given thee power and commandment to restrain it; and if He lessens the revenue, He will also shrink the necessity; or if He gives but a very little, He will make it go a great way; or if He sends thee but a coarse diet, He will bless it and make it healthful, and can cure all the anguish of thy poverty by giving thee patience and the grace of contentedness. For the grace of God secures you of provisions, and yet the grace of God feeds and supports the spirit in the want of provisions; and if a thin table be apt to enfeeble the spirits of one used to feed better, yet the cheerfulness of a spirit that is blessed will make a thin table become a delicacy, if the man was as well taught as he was fed, and learned his duty when he received the blessing. Poverty, therefore, is in some senses eligible, and to be preferred before riches; but in all senses it is very tolerable.

THE KNOWLEDGE OF GOD.

Better is it not to know at all, than not to pursue the good we know. They that know not God are infinitely far from Him; but they who know Him, and yet do not obey Him, are sometimes the nearer for their

"The Doctrine and Practice of Repentance."

knowledge, sometimes the further off, but as yet they are not arrived whither it is intended they should go.

The Religion of the Heart.

Many times God is present in the still voice and private retirements of a quiet religion and the constant spiritualities of an ordinary life, when the loud and impetuous winds, and the shining fires of more laborious and expensive actions, are profitable to others only; like a tree of balsam, distilling precious liquor for others, not for its own use. "The Great Exemplar," part i. sec. 1.

Hope.

Hope and fasting are said to be the two wings of prayer. Fasting is but as the wing of a bird; but hope is like the wing of an angel soaring up to heaven, and bears our prayers to the throne of grace. Without hope it is impossible to pray: but hope makes our prayers reasonable, passionate, and religious; for it relies upon God's promise, or experience, or providence, and story. Prayer is always in proportion to our hope, zealous and affectionate. "Holy Living," c. iv. sec. 2.

The rich mines and golden trade of both the Indies are on the other side the line: so the rich trade of hope is in the other world. Change your poor freight, which is your lading in this vessel of clay, and barter it for an immortal possession.

<small>"Christian Consolations," c. 11.</small>

HERESY.

Heresy is not an error of the understanding, but an error of the will.

<small>"Liberty of Prophesying," sec. 11.</small>

✽ ✽

Whatever an ill man believes, if he therefore believe it because it serves his own ends, be his belief true or false, the man hath an heretical mind, for to serve his own ends his mind is prepared to believe a lie. But a good man, that believes what, according to his light, and upon the use of his moral industry, he thinks true, whether he hits upon the right or no, because he hath a mind desirous of truth and prepared to believe every truth, is therefore acceptable to God, because nothing hindered him from it but what he could not help, his misery and his weakness, which being imperfections merely natural, which God never punishes, he stands fair for a blessing of his morality, which God always accepts.

<small>Ibid.</small>

Humility.

It had been impossible that Christianity should have prevailed over the wisdom and power of the Greeks and Romans, if it had not been humble to superiors, patient of injuries, charitable to the needy, a great exactor of obedience to kings, even to heathens, that they might be won and convinced; and to persecutors, that they might be sweetened in their anger or upbraided for their cruel injustice. For so doth the humble vine creep at the foot of an oak, and leans upon its lowest base, and begs shade and protection, and leave to grow under its branches, and to give and take mutual refreshment, and pay a friendly influence for a mighty patronage; and they grow and dwell together, and are the most remarkable of friends and married pairs of all the leafy nation.

<small>Sermons: "Of Christian Prudence," part ii.</small>

Whatsoever evil thou sayest of thyself, be content that others should think to be true: and if thou callest thyself fool, be not angry if another say so of thee. For if thou thinkest so truly, all men in the world desire other

<small>"Holy Living," c. ii. sec. 4.</small>

men to be of their opinion; and he is an hypocrite that accuses himself before others, with an intent not to be believed. But he that calls himself intemperate, foolish, lustful, and is angry when his neighbours call him so, is both a false and a proud person.

Love to be concealed, and little esteemed; be content to want praise, never being troubled when thou art slighted or undervalued; for thou canst not undervalue thyself, and if thou thinkest so meanly as there is reason, no contempt will seem unreasonable, and therefore it will be very tolerable.

Never be ashamed of thy birth, or thy parents, or thy trade, or thy present employment, for the meanness or poverty of any of them; and when there is an occasion to speak of them, such an occasion as would invite you to speak of anything that pleases you, omit it not, but speak as readily and indifferently of thy meanness as of thy greatness. Primislaus, the first king of Bohemia, kept his country shoes always by him, to remember from whence he was raised; and Agathocles, by the furniture of his table, confessed that from a potter he was raised to be the king of Sicily.

Make no reflex acts upon thy own humility, nor upon any other grace with which God hath enriched thy soul. For since God oftentimes hides from His saints and servants the sight of those excellent things by which they shine to others (though the dark side of the lantern be towards themselves), that he may secure the grace of humility; it is good that thou do so thyself: and if thou beholdest a grace of God in thee, remember to give Him thanks for it, that thou mayest not boast in that which is none of thy own; and consider how thou hast sullied it, by handling it with dirty fingers, with thy own imperfections, and with mixture of unhandsome circumstances. Spiritual pride is very dangerous not only by reason it spoils so many graces, by which we drew nigh unto the kingdom of God, but also because it so frequently creeps upon the spirit of holy persons. For it is no wonder for a beggar to call himself poor, or a drunkard to confess that he is no sober person; but for a holy person to be humble, for one whom all men esteem a saint to fear lest himself become a devil, and to observe his own danger, and to discern his own infirmities, and make discovery of his bad adherences, is as hard

Ibid.

as for a prince to submit himself to be guided by tutors, and make himself subject to discipline, like the meanest of his servants.

* * *

Never change thy employment for the sudden coming of another to thee ; but if modesty permits, or discretion, appear to him that visits thee the same that thou wert to God and thyself in thy privacy. But if thou wert walking or sleeping, or in any other innocent employment or retirement, snatch not up a book to seem studious, nor fall on thy knees to seem devout, nor alter anything to make him believe thee better employed than thou wert.

<small>Ibid.</small>

HYPOCRISY.

There is a universal crust of hypocrisy, that covers the face of the greatest part of mankind. Their religion consists in forms and outsides, and serves reputation or a design, but does not serve God. Their promises are but fair language, and the civilities of the piazzas or exchanges, and disband and untie like the air that beat upon their teeth, when they spake the delicious

<small>Sermons: "Of Christian Simplicity," part i.</small>

and hopeful words. Their oaths are snares to catch men, and make them confident; their contracts are arts and stratagems to deceive, measured by profit and possibility; and everything is lawful that is gainful. And their friendships are trades of getting; and their kindness of watching a dying friend is but the office of a vulture, the gaping for a legacy, the spoil of the carcass. And their sicknesses are many times policies of state; sometimes a design to show the riches of our bed-chamber. And their funeral tears are but the paranymphs and pious solicitors of a second bride. And everything that is ugly must be hid, and everything that is handsome must be seen; and that will make a fair cover for a huge deformity. And therefore it is, as they think, necessary that men should always have some pretences and forms, some faces of religion or sweetness of language, confident affirmatives or bold oaths, protracted treaties or multitude of words, affected silence or grave deportment, a good name or a good cause, a fair relation or a worthy calling, great power or a pleasant wit; anything that can be fair or that can be useful, anything that can do good or be thought good, we use it to abuse our brother, or promote our interests. Leporina resolved to die, being troubled for her husband's danger; and he resolved to die with her that had so great a kindness for him, as not to outlive the best of her husband's fortune. It was agreed; and she tempered the poison, and drank the face of the unwholesome goblet; but the weighty poison sunk to the bottom, and the easy man drank it all off, and died, and the woman carried him forth to funeral; and after a little illness, which she soon recovered, she entered upon the inheritance, and a second marriage.

INCONSIDERATION.

There is wrought upon the spirits of many men great impressions by education, by a modest and temperate nature, by human laws, and the customs and severities of sober persons, and the fears of religion, and the awfulness of a reverend man, and the several arguments and endearments of virtue: and it is not in the nature of some men to do an act in despite of reason, and religion, and arguments, and reverence, and modesty, and fear; but men are forced from their sin by the violence of the grace

<small>Sermons: "The Deceitfulness of the Heart," part ii.</small>

of God, when they hear it speak. But so a Roman gentleman kept off a whole band of soldiers, who were sent to murder him, and his eloquence was stronger than their anger and design: but, suddenly, a rude trooper rushed upon him, who neither had nor would hear him speak; and he thrust his spear into that throat whose music had charmed all his fellows into peace and gentleness. So do we. The grace of God is armour and defence enough against the most violent incursion of the spirits and the works of darkness; but then we must hear its excellent charms, and consider its reasons, and remember its precepts, and dwell with its discourses.

Purity of Intention.

Holy intention is to the actions of a man that which the soul is to the body, or form to its matter, or the root to the tree, or the sun to the world, or the fountain to a river, or the base to a pillar; for, without these, the body is a dead trunk, the matter is sluggish, the tree is a block, the world is darkness, the river is quickly dry, the pillar rushes into flatness, and a ruin; and the action is sinful, or unprofitable and

"Holy Living," c. i. sec. 2.

vain. The poor farmer that gave a dish of cold water to Artaxerxes, was rewarded with a golden goblet; and he that gives the same to a disciple in the name of a disciple, shall have a crown; but if he gives water in despite, when the disciple needs wine or a cordial, his reward shall be to want that water to cool his tongue.

THE NAME OF JESUS.

In old times, God was known by names of power, of nature, of majesty. But His name of mercy was reserved till now, when God did purpose to pour out the whole treasure of His mercy by the mediation and ministry of His holy Son. And because God gave to the holy Babe the name in which the treasures of mercy were deposited, and exalted "this name above all names," we are taught that the purpose of His counsel was to exalt and magnify His mercy above all His other works; He being delighted with this excellent demonstration of it, in the mission and manifestation and crucifixion of His Son; He hath changed the ineffable name into a name utterable by man, and desirable by all the world. This is the name which we should

"The Divine Exemplar," part i. sec. 5.

engrave in our hearts, and write upon our foreheads, and pronounce with our most harmonious accents, and rest our faith upon, and place our hopes in, and love with the overflowings of charity and joy and adoration.

THE REWARDS OF LABOUR.

Is it not labour that makes the garlic and the pulse, the sycamore and the cresses, the cheese of the goats and the butter of the sheep, to be savoury and pleasant as the flesh of the roebuck, or the milk of the kine, the marrow of oxen, or the thighs of birds? If it were not for labour, men neither could eat so much, nor relish so pleasantly, nor sleep so soundly, nor be so healthful nor so useful, so strong nor so patient, so noble nor so untempted. And as God hath made us beholden to labour for the purchase of many good things, so the thing itself owes to labour many degrees of its worth and value. And, therefore, I need not reckon that, besides these advantages, the mercies of God have found out proper and natural remedies for labour; nights to cure the sweat of the day, sleep to ease our watchfulness, rest to alleviate our burdens, and days of

Sermons: "Miracles of the Divine Mercy," part i.

religion to procure our rest: and things are so ordered that labour is become a duty and an act of many virtues, and is not so apt to turn into a sin as its contrary; and is therefore necessary, not only because we need it for making provisions for our life, but even to ease the labour of our rest; there being no greater tediousness of spirit in the world than want of employment, and an inactive life: and the lazy man is not only unprofitable but also accursed, and he groans under the load of his time, which yet passes over the active man light as a dream, or the feathers of a bird; while the unemployed is a disease, and like a long sleepless night to himself, and a load unto his country. And therefore, although in this particular, God hath been so merciful in this infliction, that from the sharpness of the curse a very great part of mankind are freed, and there are myriads of people, good and bad, who do not " eat their bread in the sweat of their brows;" yet this is but an overrunning and an excess of the Divine mercy; God did more for us than we did absolutely need: for He hath disposed of the circumstances of this curse, that man's affections are so reconciled to it that they desire it and are delighted in it; and so the anger of God is ended in loving-kindness, and the drop of water is lost in the full chalice of the wine, and the curse is gone out into a multiplied blessing.

LAODICEAN.

Saint Bernard complains of some that say, "Sufficit nobis, nolumus esse meliores quam patres nostri." (It is enough for us to be as our forefathers), who were honest and useful in their generations, but be not over-righteous. These men are such as think they have knowledge enough to need no teacher, devotion enough to need no new fires, perfection enough to need no new progress, justice enough to need no repentance; and then, because the spirit of a man, and all the things of this world, are in perpetual variety and change, these men decline, when they have gone their period; they stand still, and then revert; like a stone returning from the bosom of a cloud, where it rested as long as the thought of a child, and fell to its natural bed of earth, and dwelt below for ever.

<small>Sermons: "Of Lukewarmness and Zeal," part ii.</small>

Human Life.

A man is first a man when he comes to a certain steady use of reason, according to his proportion; and when that is, all the world of men cannot tell precisely. Some are called at age at fourteen—some at one-and-twenty—some never; but all men late enough, for the life of a man comes upon him slowly and insensibly. But as when the sun approaches towards the gates of the morning, he first opens a little eye of heaven, and sends away the spirits of darkness, and gives light to a cock, and calls up the lark to matins, and by and by gilds the fringes of a cloud, and peeps over the eastern hills, thrusting out his golden horns, like those which decked the brows of Moses when he was forced to wear a veil, because himself had seen the face of God; and still while a man tells the story, the sun gets up higher, till he shows a fair face and a full light, and then he shines one whole day, under a cloud often, and sometimes weeping great and little showers, and sets quickly: so is a man's reason and his life.

"Holy Dying," c. i. sec. 3.

THE LENGTH OF LIFE.

If we would have our life lengthened, let us begin betimes to live in the accounts of reason and sober counsels, of religion and the Spirit, and then we shall have no reason to complain that our abode on earth is so short; many men find it long enough, and, indeed, it is so to all senses. But when we spend in waste what God hath given us in plenty, when we sacrifice our youth to folly, our manhood to lust and rage, our old age to covetousness and irreligion, not beginning to live till we are to die, designing that time to virtue which indeed is infirm to everything and profitable to nothing; then we make our lives short, and lust runs away with all the vigorous and healthful part of it, and pride and animosity steal the manly portion, and craftiness and interest possess old age; *velut ex pleno et abundanti perdimus,* we spend as if we had too much time, and knew not what to do with it: we fear everything, like weak and silly mortals; and desire strangely and greedily, as if we were immortal; we complain our life is short, and yet we throw away much of it, and are weary of many

Ibid.

of its parts; we complain that the day is long, and the night is long, and we want company, and seek out arts to drive the time away, and then weep because it is gone too soon. But so the treasure of the capitol is but a small estate, when Cæsar comes to finger it, and to pay with it all his legions; and the revenue of all Egypt and the eastern provinces was but a little sum, when they were to support the luxury of Mark Antony, and feed the riot of Cleopatra; but a thousand crowns is a vast proportion to be spent in the cottage of a frugal person, or to feed an eremite. Just so is our life: it is too short to serve the ambition of a haughty prince, or an usurping rebel: too little time to purchase great wealth, to satisfy the pride of a vainglorious fool, to trample upon all the enemies of our just or unjust interest: but for the obtaining virtue, for the purchase of sobriety and modesty, for the actions of religion, God gave us time sufficient, if we make the "outgoings of the morning and evening"—that is, our infancy and old age—to be taken into the computations of a man.

The Uncertainty of Life.

Every man is born in vanity and sin. He comes into the world like morning mushrooms, soon thrusting up their heads into the air, and conversing with their kindred of the same production, and as soon they turn into dust and forgetfulness; some of them without any other interest in the affairs of the world, but that they made their parents a little glad and very sorrowful. Others ride longer in the storm; it may be until seven years of vanity be expired, and then peradventure the sun shines hot upon their heads, and they fall into the shades below, into the cover of death and darkness of the grave to hide them. But if the bubble stands the shock of a bigger drop, and outlives the chances of a child, of a careless nurse, of drowning in a pail of water, of being overlaid by a sleepy servant, or such little accidents, then the young man dances like a bubble, empty and gay, and shines like a dove's neck, or the image of a rainbow, which hath no substance, and whose very imagery and colours are fantastical; and so he dances out the gaiety of his youth, and is all the while in a storm, and endures only because he is not knocked on

Ibid. c. i. sec. 1.

the head by a drop of bigger rain, or crushed by the pressure of a load of indigested meat, or quenched by the disorder of an ill-placed humour; and to preserve a man alive in the midst of so many chances and hostilities, is as great a miracle as to create him, to preserve him from rushing into nothing, and at first to draw him up from nothing, were equally the issues of an Almighty power.

DEATH IN LIFE.

Let us cast our eyes upon our life past; let us consider what is become of our infancy, childhood, and youth; they are now dead in us; in the same manner shall those ages of our life, which are to come, die also. Neither do we only die in the principal times of life, but every hour, every moment, includes a kind of death in the succession and change of things. What content is there in life, which dies not by some succeeding sorrow? What affliction of pain, which is not followed by some equal, or greater grief than itself! Why are we grieved for what is absent, since it offends us being present? What we desire with impatience, being possessed, brings care and solicitude, grief and affliction.

<small>"Contemplations of the State of Man," book i. c. 1.</small>

The short time which any pleasure stays with us, it is not to be enjoyed wholly, and all at once, but tasted by parts; so as, when the second part comes, we feel not the pleasure of the first, lessening itself every moment, and we ourselves still dying with it, there being no instant of life wherein death gains not ground of us; the motion of the heavens is but the swift turn of the spindle, which rolls up the thread of our lives; and a most fleet horse, upon which death runs post after us. There is no moment of life wherein death hath not equal jurisdiction; and there is no point of life which we divide not with death; so as, if well considered, we live but only one point, and have not life but for the present instant. Our years past are now vanished, and we enjoy no more of them than if we were already dead; the years to come we live not, and possess no more of them than if we were not yet born; yesterday is gone, to-morrow we know not what shall be; of to-day many hours are past, and we live them not; others are to come, and whether we shall live them or no is uncertain; so that, all counts cast up, we live but this present moment; and in this also we are dying; so that we cannot say that life is anything but the half of an instant, an indivisible point divided betwixt it and death.

※ ※

Guerricus, a most famous divine, hearing the fifth chapter of Genesis read, wherein are recounted the sons and descendants of Adam, in these terms: "The whole life of Adam was nine hundred and thirty years, and he died; the life of his son, Seth, was nine hundred and twelve years, and he died," and so of the rest, began to think with himself, that if such and so great men, after so long time, ended in death, it was not safe to lose more time in this world, but so to secure his life that, losing it here, he might find it hereafter. What can the delights of man be since his life is but a dream, a shadow, and as the twinkling of an eye? If the most long life be short, what can be the pleasures of that moment by which is lost eternal happiness? Oh, how vain are men, who, seeing life so short, endeavour to live long, and not to live well! Since it is a thing most certain that every man may live well, but no man, what age soever he attains unto, can live long; every day we die, and every day we lose some part of life; and in our

Ibid.

growth, our life decreases and grows less ; and this very day wherein we live, we divide with death. Our life, in the Book of Wisdom, is compared unto the passing of a shadow, which as it may be said to be a kind of night, so life may be called a kind of death ; for, as the shadow hath some part of light, some of darkness, so our life hath some part of death, and some of life, until it comes to end in a pure death ; and since it is to end in a not being, it is very little to be regarded, especially compared with eternity, which hath a being constant and for ever. The shadow, wheresoever it passes, leaves no track behind it ; and of the greatest personages in the world when they are once dead, then there remains no more than if they had never lived. How many preceding emperors in the Assyrian monarchy were lords of the world as well as Alexander? And now we remain not only ignorant of their monuments, but know not so much as their names ; and of the same great Alexander, what have we at this day except the vain noise of his fame? There is nothing constant in this life ; the moon hath every month her changes, but the life of man hath them every day, every hour ; now he is sick, now in health, now sorrowful, now merry, now fearful. With what imaginations is he afflicted! With how many labours and toils does he daily wrestle! With what thoughts and apprehensions doth he torment himself! What dangers of soul and body doth he run into! What vanity is he forced to behold! What injuries to suffer! What necessities and afflictions! Nay, such is our whole life, that it seems unto me little less evil than that of hell, but only for the hope we have of heaven; our infancy is full of ignorance and fears, our youth of sin, our age of sorrow, and our whole life of dangers. There is none content with his condition, but he who will die whilst he lives; insomuch as life cannot be good unless it most resemble death. Since, therefore, the whole time of this life is so short, and we know not how long it will last, let us resolve not to lose the opportunity of gaining eternity.

LOVE.

Love is the greatest thing that God can give us, for Himself is love, and it is the greatest thing we can give to God, for it will also give ourselves, and carry with it all that is ours. The apostle calls it the band of perfection;

"Holy Living," c. iv. sec. 3.

it is the old, and it is the new, and it is the great commandment, and it is all the commandments; for it is the fulfilling of the law.

The sum is this: no Christian does his duty to God but he that serves Him with all his heart: and although it becomes us to fulfil all righteousness, even the external also, yet that which makes us gracious in His eyes is not the external, it is the love of the heart and the real change of the mind and obedience of the spirit; that is the first great measure of the righteousness evangelical.

<small>Sermons: "The Righteousness Evangelical described."</small>

Love is the soul of Christianity, and suffering is the soul of love.

<small>Sermons: "Faith and Patience of the Saints," part ii.</small>

MARRIAGE.

Marriage is the nursery of heaven; the virgin sends prayers to God, but she carries but one soul to Him; but the state of marriage fills up the numbers of the elect, and hath in it the labour of love and the delicacies of friendship, the blessing of society, and the union of

<small>Sermons: "The Marriage Ring," part i.</small>

hands and hearts; it hath in it less of beauty, but more of safety, than the single life; it hath more care, but less danger; it is more merry, and more sad; is fuller of sorrows, and fuller of joys; it lies under more burdens, but it is supported by all the strengths of love and charity, and those burdens are delightful.

※ ※

Let the husband and wife infinitely avoid a curious distinction of mine and thine, for this hath caused all the laws, and all the suits, and all the wars in the world; let them, who have but one person, have also but one interest.

Ibid.

It is an ill band of affections to tie two hearts together by a little thread of red and white. And they can love no longer but until the next ague comes; and they are fond of each other but at the chance of fancy, or the smallpox, or child-bearing, or care, or time, or anything that can destroy a pretty flower.

Ibid.

Man and wife are equally concerned to avoid all

offences of each other in the beginning of their conversation; every little thing can blast an infant blossom, and the breath of the south can shake the little rings of the vine when first they begin to curl like the locks of a new-weaned boy; but when by age and consolidation they stiffen into the hardness of a stem, and have, by the warm embraces of the sun and the kisses of heaven, brought forth their clusters, they can endure the storms of the north and the loud noises of a tempest, and yet never be broken; so are the early unions of an unfixed marriage; watchful and observant, jealous and busy, inquisitive and careful, and apt to take alarm at every unkind word. *Ibid.*

Marriage is the queen of friendships, in which there is a communication of all that can be communicated by friendship, and it being made sacred by vows and love, by bodies and souls, by interest and custom, by religion and by laws, by common counsels and common fortunes; it is the principal in the kind of friendship, and the measure of all the rest. *"The Measures and Offices of Friendship."*

MEDITATION.

"The Great Exemplar," part i. sec. 5. Meditation is an act of the understanding put to the right use.

A garden that is watered with short and sudden showers is more uncertain in its fruits and beauties than if a rivulet waters it with a perpetual distilling and constant humectation. And just such are the short emissions and unpremeditated resolutions of piety, begotten by a dash of holy rain from heaven, whereby God sometimes uses to call the careless but to taste what excellencies of piety they neglect; but if they be not produced by the reason of religion and the philosophy of meditation they have but the life of a fly or a tall gourd, they come into the world only to say they had a being; you could scarce know their length but by measuring the ground they cover in their fall.

Ibid.

⁂

Meditations in order to a good life, let them be as exalted as the capacity of the person and subject will endure up to the height of contemplation, but if contemplation comes to be a distinct thing, and something

Ibid.

besides or beyond a distinct degree of virtuous meditation, it is lost to all sense and religion and prudence. Let no man be hasty to eat of the fruits of paradise before his time.

※ ※ ※

If, in the definition of meditation, I should call it an unaccustomed and unpractised duty, I should speak a truth, though somewhat in artificially : for not only the interior beauties and brighter excellencies are as unfelt as ideas and abstractions are, but also the practice and common knowledge of the duty itself are strangers to us, like the retirements of the deep or the undiscovered treasures of the Indian hills. And this is a very great cause of the dryness and expiration of men's devotion, because our souls are so little refreshed with the waters and holy dews of meditation. We go to our prayers by chance or order or by determination of accidental occurrences, and we recite them as we read a book, and sometimes we are sensible of the duty, and a flash of lightning makes the room bright, and our prayers end, and the lightning is gone, and we as dark as ever. We draw our water

Ibid.

from standing pools which never are filled but with sudden showers, and therefore we are dry so often; whereas if we should draw water from the fountains of our Saviour, and derive them through the channel of diligent and prudent meditations, our devotion would be a continual current, and safe against the barrenness of frequent droughts.

※ ※ ※

Meditation is the duty of all, and therefore God hath fitted such matter for it which is proportioned to every understanding; and the greatest mysteries of Christianity are plainest, and yet most fruitful of meditation, and most useful to the production of piety. High speculations are as barren as the tops of cedars; but the fundamentals of Christianity are fruitful as the valleys or the creeping vine.

<small>Ibid.</small>

CHRIST'S MARTYRS.

He that overcomes his fear of death does well, but if he hath not also overcome his lust or his anger his baptism of blood will not wash him clean. Many things may make a man willing to die in a good cause;—public reputation, hope of reward, gallantry

<small>Sermons: "The Faith and Patience of the Saints," part iii.</small>

of spirit, a confident resolution, and a masculine courage ; or a man may be vexed into a stubborn and unrelenting suffering ; but nothing can make a man live well but the grace and the love of God. But those persons are infinitely condemned by their last act who profess their religion to be worth dying for, and yet are so unworthy as not to live according to its institution. It were a rare felicity if every good cause could be managed by good men only, but we have found that evil men have spoiled a good cause, but never that a good cause made those evil men good and holy. If the governor of Samaria had crucified Simon Magus for receiving Christian baptism he had no more died a martyr than he lived a saint. For dying is not enough, and dying in a good cause is not enough ; but then only we receive the crown of martyrdom when our death is the seal of our life, and our life is a continual testimony of our duty, and both give testimony to the excellences of the religion, and glorify the grace of God. If a man be gold the fire purges him, but it burns him if he be, like stubble, cheap, light, and useless ; for martyrdom is the consummation of love.

There are many who would die for Christ if they were put to it and yet will not quit a lust for Him; those are hardly to be esteemed Christ's martyrs; unless they be "dead unto sin" their dying for an article, or a good action, will not pass the great scrutiny. And it may be boldness of spirit, or sullenness, or an honourable gallantry of mind, or something that is excellent in civil and political estimate, moves the person, and endears the suffering; but that love only "which keeps the commandments" will teach us to die for love, and from love to pass to blessedness through the red sea of blood.

<small>"The Great Exemplar," part ii. sec. 12.</small>

Nursing Children.

That religion which commands us to visit and to tend sick strangers, and wash the feet of the poor, and dress their ulcers, and sends us upon charitable embassies into unclean prisons, and bids us lay down our lives for one another, is not pleased with a niceness and sensual curiosity which denies suck to our own children. What is more humane and affectionate than Christianity? and what is less natural and

<small>"The Great Exemplar," part i. sec. 3.</small>

charitable than to deny the expresses of a mother's affection? which certainly to good women is the greatest trouble in the world, and the greatest violence to their desires, if they should not express and minister. And it would be considered whether those mothers who have neglected their first duties of piety and charity can expect so prompt and easy returns of duty and piety from their children, whose best foundation is love, and that love strongest which is most natural, and that most natural which is conveyed by the first ministries and impresses of nourishment and education. And if love descends more strongly than it ascends, and commonly falls from the parents upon the children in cataracts and returns back again up to the parents but in gentle dews; if the child's affection keeps the same proportions towards such unkind mothers, it will be as little as atoms in the sun, and never express itself but when the mother needs it not ; that is, in the sunshine of a clear fortune. This, then, is amongst those instincts which are natural, heightened first by reason, and then exalted by grace into the obligation of a law ; and, being amongst the sanctions of nature, its prevarication is a crime very near those sins, which divines, in detestation of their malignity, call sins against nature, and is never to be excused but in cases of necessity.

OBEDIENCE.

Remember that the assurance of blessing and health and salvation is not made by doing what we list, or being where we desire, but by doing God's will and being in the place of His appointment. We may be safe in Egypt if we be there in obedience to God, and we may perish among the babes of Bethlehem if we be there by our own election.

<small>Ibid. part i. sec. 6.</small>

RESTRAINT OF OPINION.

Force in matters of opinion can do no good, but is very apt to do hurt, for no man can change his opinion when he will, or be satisfied in his reason that his opinion is false, because discountenanced. If a man could change his opinion when he lists he might cure many inconveniences of his life; all his fears and his sorrows would soon disband if he would but alter his opinion, whereby he is persuaded that such an accident that afflicts him is an evil, and such an

<small>"Liberty of Prophesying," sec. 13.</small>

object formidable ; let him but believe himself impregnable, or that he receives a benefit when he is plundered, disgraced, imprisoned, condemned, and afflicted, neither his steps need to be disturbed nor his quietness discomposed. But if a man cannot change his opinion when he lists, nor ever does heartily or resolutely but when he cannot do otherwise, then to use force may make him a hypocrite, but never to be a right believer ; and so, instead of erecting a trophy to God and true religion, we build a monument for the devil.

The Peace of God.

That is not peace from above, to have all things according to our human and natural wishes ; but to be in favour with God, that is peace ; always remembering that to be chastised by Him is not a certain testimony of His mere wrath, but to all His servants a character of love and of paternal provision, since "He chastises every son whom He receives." Whosoever seeks to avoid all this world's adversity can never find peace ; but he only who hath resolved all his affections, and placed them in the heart of God ; he who denies his own will, and

"The Great Exemplar," part i. sec. 4.

hath killed self-love, and all those enemies within, that make afflictions to become miseries indeed, and full of bitterness ; he only enjoys this peace : and in proportion to every man's mortification and self-denial, so are the degrees of his peace.

※

Here we labour, but receive no benefit ; we sow many times, and reap not ; or reap, and do not gather in ; or gather in, and do not possess ; or possess, but do not enjoy ; or if we enjoy, we are still unsatisfied, it is with anguish of spirit, and circumstances of vexation. A great heap of riches makes neither our clothes warm, nor our meat more nutritive, nor our beverage more pleasant ; and it feeds the eye, but never fills it, but, like drink to an hydropic person, increases the thirst and promotes the torment. But the grace of God, though but like a grain of mustard-seed, fills the furrows of the heart ; and as the capacity increases, itself grows up in equal degrees, and never suffers any emptiness or dissatisfaction, but carries content and fulness all the way ; and the degrees of augmentation are not steps and near approaches to satisfaction, but increasings of the capacity ; the soul is satisfied

Ibid. part ii. sec. 12.

all the way, and receives more, not because it wanted any, but that it can now hold more, is more receptive of felicities. And in every minute of sanctification there is so excellent a condition of joy and high satisfaction, that the very calamities, the afflictions, and persecutions of the world, are turned into felicities by the activity of the prevailing ingredient; like a drop of water falling into a tun of wine, it is ascribed into a new family, losing its own nature by a conversion into the more noble. For now that all passionate desires are dead, and there is nothing remanent that is vexatious, the peace, the serenity, the quiet sleeps, the evenness of spirit, and contempt of things below, remove the soul from all neighbourhood of displeasure, and place it at the foot of the throne, whither when it is ascended, it is possessed of felicities eternal.

CHRISTIAN PHILOSOPHY.

Aristotle and Porphyry, and the other Greek philosophers, studied the heavens, to search out their natural causes and production of bodies; the wiser Chaldees and Assyrians studied the same things, that they

Ibid., part i. sec. 5.

might learn their influences upon us, and make predictions of contingencies ; the more moral Egyptian described his theorems in hieroglyphics and fantastic representments, to teach principles of policy, economy, and other prudences of morality and secular negotiation : but the same philosophy, when it is made Christian, considers as they did, but to greater purposes, even that from the book of the creatures we may glorify the Creator, and hence derive arguments of worship and religion : this is Christian philosophy.

Practical Piety.

If men would a little turn the tables, and be as zealous for a good life, and all the strictest precepts of Christianity (which is a religion the most holy, the most reasonable, and the most consummate that ever was taught to man), as they are for such propositions in which neither the life nor the ornament of Christianity is concerned, we should find that, as a consequent of this piety, men would be as careful as they could to find out all truths, and the sense of all revelations which may concern their duty ; and where men were miserable

"Liberty of Prophesying," The Epistle Dedicatory.

and could not, yet others that lived good lives too, would also be so charitable as not to add affliction to this misery: and both of them are parts of good life. To be compassionate, and to help to bear one another's burdens, not to destroy the weak, but to entertain him meekly, that is a precept of charity; and to endeavour to find out the whole will of God, that also is a part of the obedience, the choice and the excellency of faith: and he lives not a good life that does not do both these.

ANCESTRAL PIETY.

As the root of a tree receives nourishment not only sufficient to preserve its own life, but to transmit a plastic juice to the trunk of the tree, and from thence to the utmost branch and smallest germ that knots in the most distant part, so shall the great and exemplar piety of the father of a family not only preserve to the interest of his own soul the life of grace and hopes of glory, but shall be a quickening spirit, active and communicative of a blessing, not only to the trunk of the tree, to the body and rightly-descending line, but even to

Sermons: "The Entail of Curses Cut off," part ii.

the collateral branches, to the most distant relatives, and all that shall claim a kindred, shall have a title to a blessing.

HOLY PLACES.

God is, by grace and benediction, specially present in holy places, and in the solemn assemblies of His servants. If holy people meet in grots and dens of the earth when persecution or a public necessity disturbs the public order, circumstance, and convenience, God fails not to come thither to them: but God is also, by the same or a greater reason, present there, where they meet ordinarily, by order, and public authority; there God is present ordinarily, that is, at every such meeting. God will go out of His way to meet His saints, when themselves are forced out of their way of order by a sad necessity; but else, God's usual way is to be present in those places where His servants are appointed ordinarily to meet. But His presence there signifies nothing but a readiness to hear their prayers, to bless their persons, to accept their offices, and to like even the circumstance of orderly and public meeting. For thither the

"Holy Living," c. i. sec. 3.

prayers of consecration, the public authority separating it, and God's love of order, and the reasonable customs of religion, have, in ordinary, and in a certain degree, fixed this manner of His presence; and He loves to have it so.

※ ※

I consider that those riches and beauties in churches and religious solemnities, which add nothing to God, add much devotion to us and much honour and efficacy to devotion. *"The Great Exemplar," part ii. sec. 11.* For since impression is made upon the soul by the intervening of corporal things, our religion and devotion of the soul receives the addition of many degrees by such instruments. Insomuch that we see persons of the greatest fancy, and such who are most pleased with outward fairnesses, are most religious. Great understandings make religion lasting and reasonable; but great fancies make it more scrupulous, strict, operative, and effectual. And therefore it is strange that we shall bestow such great expenses to make our own houses convenient and delectable, that we may entertain ourselves with complacency and appetite, and yet think that religion is not worth the ornament, nor our fancies fit to be carried into the choice and prosecution of religious actions, with sweetness, entertainments, and fair propositions. If we say that God is not the better for a rich house or a costly service, we may also remember that neither are we the better for rich clothes; and the sheep will keep us as modest, as warm, and as clean as the silk-worm; and a gold chain or a carkenet of pearl does no more contribute to our happiness than it does to the service of religion. For if we reply that they help to the esteem and reputation of our persons, and the distinction of them from the vulgar, from the servants of the lot of Issachar, and add reverence and veneration to us, how great a shame is it if we study by great expenses to get reputation and accidental advantages to ourselves, and not by the same means to purchase reverence and esteem to religion; since we see that religion, amongst persons of ordinary understandings, receives as much external and accidental advantages by the accession of exterior ornaments and accommodation, as we ourselves can by rich clothes and garments of wealth, ceremony, and distinction. And as in princes' courts the reverence to princes is quickened and increased by an outward state and glory, so also it is in the service of God.

THE PILGRIM'S PROGRESS.

Here thou art but a stranger travelling to thy country, where the glories of a kingdom are prepared for thee; it is therefore a huge folly to be much afflicted because thou hast a less convenient inn to lodge in by the way. <small>"Holy Living," c. ii. sec 6.</small>

* *

The things of this world are not only a shadow, but are very deceitful; they promise us goods, and give us evils; promise us ease, and give us cares; promise security, and give us danger; promise us great contents, and give us great vexations; there is no felicity upon earth, no happiness which mounts so high, which is not depressed by some low calamity: it is not needful to attend the end of life to see the imposture of it, it is enough to see the alterations whilst it lasts; be assured that vain is all the greatness of the earth if that of heaven be not gained by it. Since, then, all kingdoms, empires, honours, and greatness whatsoever are but a <small>"Contemplations of the State of Man," book i. c. 2.</small>

shadow, and will presently vanish, and we are here in this world but as in an inn, from whence we are suddenly to depart, let us take care for our journey and furnish ourselves with provision and a viaticum for eternity; let us clothe ourselves with such garments as we may carry along with us. This may be our comfort, that our wealth, whether we will or no, may be taken from us, but eternal happiness, unless by our fault, cannot; we may be deprived of honours against our wills, but not of our virtues, except we consent; temporal goods may perish, be stolen, and lost many ways, but spiritual goods can only be forsaken, and are then only lost when we leave them by our sins; the roses of glory in heaven do never fade, nor doth custom dull the lively taste of those celestial delights; let us therefore convey our riches here through the hands of the poor in bills of exchange into the eternity of glory, where such money is current, for our good works will follow us. I will therefore preserve myself in humility, I will not confide in prosperity, nor presume upon my virtues, though never so great, since every man is subject to fall into those misfortunes he little thinks of. I will not trust in life, because it may fail, whilst the goods of it remain; and will as little trust in them, because they may likewise fail, whilst it continues.

Riches were invented for the ease and commodity of life; but as man hath made them, they serve for the greatest trouble and vexation: he who hath wealth hath most want, because he not only needs for himself, but for all which he possesseth: so that he which hath a great house hath the same necessities that his house hath, which are many; for a great house requires much furniture and a large family; and so charges the master with multitudes of servants, great quantities of plate, hangings, and other ornaments superfluous to use and human commodity; insomuch as none are more poor than the rich, because they want, not only for themselves, but for all that is theirs. At least, riches want not this incommodity, that although they were invented for human use and ease, yet he that hath them in the greatest abundance hath the greatest cares, troubles, dangers, and ever the greatest losses. Let us, therefore, while we have time, make over our riches; let us send them before us into another

Ibid., c. 111.

world; heaven stands open to receive them, we need not doubt of safe carriage; the carriers are very faithful and trusty—they are the poor and needy of this world; we make over unto them here, by way of exchange, a few things of little value; being to receive in heaven for them, an exceeding eternal weight of glory.

The Rewards of Poverty.

Poverty is the sister of a good mind; it ministers aid to wisdom, industry to our spirit, severity to our thoughts, soberness to our counsels, modesty to our desires; it restrains extravagancy and dissolution of appetites; the next thing above our present condition, which is commonly the object of our wishes, being temperate and little, proportionable enough to nature, not wandering beyond the limits of necessity or a moderate conveniency, or, at farthest, but to a free refreshment and recreation. And the cares of poverty are single and mean, rather a fit employment to correct our levities than a business to impede our better thoughts; since a little thing supplies the needs of nature, and the earth and the

"The Great Exemplar," part ii. sec. 12.

fountain with little trouble minister food to us, and God's common providence and daily dispensation eases the cares and makes them portable. But the cares and businesses of rich men are violences to our whole man; they are loads of memory, business for the understanding, work for two or three arts and sciences, employment for many servants to assist in, increase the appetite, and heighten the thirst; and, by making their dropsy bigger and their capacities large, they destroy all those opportunities and possibilities of charity in which only riches can be useful. But it is not a mere poverty of possession which entitles us to the blessing, but a poverty of spirit, that is, a contentedness in every state, an aptness to renounce all when we are obliged in duty, a refusing to continue a possession when we for it must quit a virtue or a noble action; a divorce of our affections from those gilded vanities; a generous contempt of the world, and at no hand heaping riches, either with injustice or with avarice, either with wrong or impotency of action or affection.

Prayer.

Short passes, quick ejections, concise forms and remembrances, holy breathings, prayers like little posies, may be sent forth without number on every occasion, and God will note them in His book. But all that have a care to walk with God fill their vessels more largely as soon as they rise, before they begin the work of the day, and before they lie down again at night: which is to observe what the Lord appointed in the Levitical ministry, a morning and an evening lamb to be laid upon the altar. So with them that are not stark irreligious, prayer is the key to open the day, and the bolt to shut in the night. But as the skies drop the early dew and the evening dew upon the grass, yet it would not spring and grow green by that constant and double falling of the dew unless some great showers, at certain seasons, did supply the rest; so the customary devotion of prayer, twice a day, is the falling of the early and the latter dew; but if you will increase and flourish in the works of grace, empty the great clouds sometimes, and let them fall into a full shower of prayer: choose out

"Christian Consolations," c. iv.

the seasons in your own discretion, when prayer shall overflow, like Jordan in the time of harvest.

※

Converse with God by frequent prayer. In particular, desire that your desires may be right, and love to have your affections regular and holy. To which purpose, make very frequent addresses to God by ejaculations and communions, and an assiduous daily devotion; discover to Him all your wants; complain to Him of all your affronts; do as Hezekiah did, lay your misfortunes and your ill news before Him, spread them before the Lord; call to Him for health, run to Him for counsel, beg of Him for pardon; and it is as natural to love Him to whom we make such addresses, and of whom we have such dependencies, as it is for children to love their parents.

"Holy Living," c. iv. sec. 3.

※

Desire what you pray for; for certain it is you will pray passionately if you desire fervently. Prayers are but the body of the bird; desires are its angel's wings.

"The Worthy Communicant," c. ii. sec. 4.

※

The rule is easy: whatsoever you need, ask it of God so long as you want it, even till you have it. For God, therefore, many times defers to grant, that thou mayest persevere to ask; and because every holy prayer is a glorification of God by the confessing many of His attributes, a lasting and a persevering prayer is a little image of the hallelujahs and services of eternity; it is a continuation to do that, according to our measures, which we shall be doing to eternal ages: therefore, think not that five or six hearty prayers can secure to thee a great blessing, and a supply of a mighty necessity. He that prays so, and then leaves off, hath said some prayers, and done the ordinary offices of his religion, but hath not secured the blessing, nor used means reasonably proportionable to a mighty interest.

Sermons: "The Return of Prayers," part ii.

※

There is no greater argument in the world of our spiritual weakness, and the falseness of our hearts in matters of religion, than the backwardness which most men have always, and all men have sometimes, to say their prayers; so weary of their length, so

Sermons: "The Deceitfulness of the Heart," part i.

glad when they are done, so witty to excuse and frustrate an opportunity: and yet there is no manner of trouble in the duty, no weariness of bones, no violent labours; nothing but begging a blessing, and receiving it; nothing but doing ourselves the greatest honour of speaking to the greatest person, and greatest King of the world: and, that we should be unwilling to do this, so unable to continue in it, so backward to return to it, so without gust and relish in the doing it, can have no visible reason in the nature of the thing, but something within us, a strange sickness in the heart, a spiritual nauseating or loathing of manna, something that hath no name; but we are sure it comes from a weak, a faint, and false heart.

The words of prayer are no part of the Spirit of prayer; words may be the body of it, but the Spirit of prayer always consists in holiness, that is, in holy desires and holy actions. Words are not properly capable of being holy; all words are in themselves servants of things; and the holiness of a prayer is not at all concerned in the manner of its expres-

<small>Sermons: "Of the Spirit of Grace," part ii.</small>

sion, but in the spirit of it; that is, in the violence of its desires, and the innocence of its ends and the continuance of its employment.

※

If you will know how it is with you in the matter of your prayers, examine whether or no the form of your prayer be the rule of your life. Every petition to God is a precept to man; and when, in your litanies, you pray to be delivered from malice and hypocrisy, from pride and envy, from fornication and every deadly sin, all that is but a line of duty, and tells us that we must never consent to an act of pride, or a thought of envy, to a temptation of uncleanness, or the besmearings and evil paintings of hypocrisy. But we, when we pray against a sin, think we have done enough; and if we ask for a grace, suppose there is no more required. Now prayer is an instrument of help, a procuring auxiliaries of God, that we may do our duty; and why should we ask for help, if we be not ourselves bound to do the thing?

<small>"The Worthy Communicant," c. ii. sec. 4.</small>

Whatever we beg of God, let us also work for

it, if the thing be matter of duty or a consequent to industry. For God loves to bless labour and to reward it, but not to support idleness. And therefore our blessed Saviour in His sermons joins watchfulness with prayer; for God's graces are but assistances, not new creations of the whole habit, in every instant or period of our life. Read Scriptures, and then pray to God for understanding. Pray against temptation; but you must also resist the devil and then he will flee from you. Ask of God competency of living; but you must also work with your hands the things that are honest, that ye may have to supply in time of need. We can but do our endeavour, and pray for a blessing, and then leave the success with God; and beyond this we cannot deliberate, we cannot take care— but so far we must.

<small>"Holy Living," c. iv. sec. 7.</small>

We usually judge of the well or ill of our devotions and services, by what we feel; and we think God rewards everything in the present, and by proportion to our own expectations; and if we feel a present rejoicing of spirit

<small>"The Great Exemplar," part i. sec. 7.</small>

all is well with us; the smoke of the sacrifice ascended right in a holy cloud: but if we feel nothing of comfort, then we count it a prodigy and ominous, and we suspect ourselves; and most commonly we have reason. Such irradiations of cheerfulness are always welcome; but it is not always anger that takes them away: the cloud removed from before the camp of Israel, and stood before the host of Pharaoh; but this was a design of ruin to the Egyptians and of security to Israel: and, if those bright angels that go with us to direct our journeys, remove out of our sight, and stand behind us, it is not always an argument that the anger of the Lord is gone out against us; but such decays of sense and clouds of spirit are excellent conservators of humility and restrain those intemperances and vainer thoughts which we are prompted to in the gaiety of our spirits.

※ ※

God's blessings, though they come infallibly, yet not always speedily, saving only that it is a blessing to be delayed, that we may increase our desire, and renew our prayers, and do acts of confidence and patience, and ascertain and

Ibid., part ii. sec. 12.

increase the blessing when it comes. For we do not more desire to be blessed than God does to hear us importunate for blessing, and He weighs every sigh, and bottles up every tear, and records every prayer, and looks through the cloud with delight to see us upon our knees, and, when He sees His time, His light breaks through it and shines upon us. Only we must not make our accounts for God according to the course of the sun, but the measures of eternity. He measures us by our needs, and we must not measure Him by our impatience. "God is not slack, as some men count slackness," saith the apostle; and we find it so when we have waited long. All the elapsed time is no part of the tediousness; the trouble of it is past with itself and for the future we know not how little it may be; for aught we know, we are already entered into the cloud that brings the blessing. However, pray till it comes, for we shall never miss to receive our desire if it be holy, or innocent, and safe; or else we are sure of a great reward of our prayers.

Desire is the life of prayer, and if you indeed desire what you pray for, you will also labour for what you desire; and if you find it otherwise with yourselves, your coming to church is but like the Pharisees going up to the temple to pray. If your heart be not present, neither will God, and then there is a sound of men and women between a pair of dead walls from whence, because neither God nor your souls are present, you must needs go home without a blessing.

Sermons: "The Righteousness Evangelical Described."

* *

Anger is a perfect alienation of the mind from prayer, and therefore is contrary to that attention which presents our prayers in a right line to God. For so have I seen a lark rising from his bed of grass, and soaring upwards, singing as he rises, and hopes to get to heaven, and climb above the clouds; but the poor bird was beaten back with the loud sighings of an eastern wind, and his motion made irregular and inconstant, descending more at every breath of the tempest than it could recover by the libration and frequent weighing of his wings till the little creature

Sermons: "The Return of Prayers," part ii.

was forced to sit down and pant and stay till the storm was over; and then it made a prosperous flight, and did rise and sing, as if it had learned music and motion from an angel as he passed sometimes through the air about his ministries here below. So is the prayer of a good man; when his affairs have required business, and his business was matter of discipline, and his discipline was to pass upon a sinning person, or had a design of charity, his duty met with infirmities of a man, and anger was its instrument, and the instrument became stronger than the prime agent, and raised a tempest and overruled the man; and then his prayer was broken, and his thoughts were troubled, and his words went up towards a cloud, and his thoughts pulled them back again and made them without intention; and the good man sighs for his infirmity, but must be content to lose the prayer, and he must recover it when his anger is removed and his spirit is becalmed, and then it ascends to heaven upon the wings of the holy dove, and dwells with God, till it returns, like the useful bee, laden with a blessing and the dew of heaven.

Vain Prayers.

There are many things in our prayer which we ask for and do not know what to do with if we had them, and we do not feel any want of them, and we care not whether we have them or no. We ask for the Spirit of God, for wisdom, and for a right judgment in all things, and yet there are not many in our Christian assemblies who use to trouble themselves at all with judging concerning the mysteries of godliness. Men pray for humility, and yet at the same time think that all that which is indeed humility is a pitiful poorness of spirit, pusillanimity, and want of good breeding. We pray for a contrition and a broken heart, and yet, if we chance to be melancholy, we long to be comforted, and think that the lectures of the cross bring death, and, therefore, are not the way of eternal life. We pray sometimes that God may be first and last in all our thoughts, and yet we conceive it no great matter whether He be or no; but we are sure that He is not, but the things of the world do take up the place of God, and yet we hope to be saved for all that, and, consequently, are very indifferent concerning the

"The Worthy Communicant," c. ii. sec. 4.

return of that prayer. We frequently call upon God for His grace that we may never fall into sin ; now in this, besides that we have no hopes to be heard, and think it impossible to arrive to a state of life in which we shall not commit sins, yet if we do sin we know there is a remedy so ready that we believe we are not much the worse if we do. Here are prayers enough ; but where are the desires all this while? We pray against covetousness, and pride, and gluttony ; but nothing that we do but is either covetousness or pride ; so that our prayers are terminated upon a word, not upon a thing. We do covetous actions, and speak proud words, and have high thoughts, and do not passionately desire to have affections contrary to them, but only to such notions of the sin as we have entertained, which are such as will do no real prejudice or mortification to the sin ; and whatever our prayers are, yet it is certain our desires are so little, and so content with anything of this nature, that for very many spiritual petitions we are indifferent whether they be granted or not.

RECREATION.

Let not your recreations be lavish spenders of your time, but choose such which are healthful, short, transient, recreative, and apt to refresh you; but at no hand dwell upon them or make them your great employment, for he that spends his time in sports and calls it recreation is like him whose garment is all made of fringes and his meat nothing but sauces; they are healthless, chargeable, and useless. And therefore avoid such games which require much time or long attendance, or which are apt to steal thy affections from more severe employments. For to whatsoever thou hast given thy affections, thou wilt not grudge to give thy time. Natural necessity and the example of St. John, who recreated himself with sporting with a tame partridge, teach us that it is lawful to relax and unbend our bow, but not to suffer it to be unready or unstrung.

"Holy Living," c. i. sec. 1.

RELIGION.

A man talks of religon but as of a dream, and from thence he awakens into the businesses of the world, and acts them deliberately, with perfect action and full resolution, and contrives, and considers, and lives in them; but when he falls asleep again, or is taken from the scene of his own employment and choice, then he dreams again, and religion makes such impressions as is the conversation of a dreamer, and he acts accordingly. Sermons: "The Deceitful-ness of the Heart," part ii.

※ ※

We dress ourselves upon a day of religion, and then we cannot endure to think on sin; and if we do, we sigh, and when we sigh we pray, and suppose that if we might die upon that day it would be a good day's work, for we could not die in a better time. But let us not deceive ourselves. That is our picture that is like us every day in the week; and if you are as just in your buying and selling as you are when you are saying your prayers; if you are as chaste in your conversation as you are in your religious retirement; if your temperance be the same every day as it is "The Worthy Communicant," c. ii. sec. 3.

in your thoughts upon a fasting-day ; if you wear the same habits of virtue every day in the week as you put on upon a communion-day—you have more reason to think yourselves prepared than by all the extempore piety and solemn religion that rises at the sound of a bell and keeps her time by the calendar of the Church more than by the laws of God.

※

We make religion to be the work of a few hours in the whole year ; we are without fancy or affection to the severities of holy living ; we reduce religion to the believing of a few articles, and doing nothing that is considerable ; we pray seldom, and then but very coldly and indifferently ; we communicate not so often as the sun salutes both the tropics ; we profess Christ, but dare not die for Him ; we are factious for a religion, and will not live according to its precepts ; we call ourselves Christians, and love to be ignorant of many of the laws of Christ, lest our knowledge should force us into shame, or into the troubles of a holy life.

Sermons: "The Deceitfulness of the Heart," part ii.

He that does his recreation or his merchandise cheerfully, promptly, readily, and busily, and the works of religion slowly, flatly, and without appetite, and the spirit moves like Pharaoh's chariots when the wheels were off, it is a sign that his heart is not right with God, but it cleaves too much to the world.

"Holy Living," c. i. sec. 2.

* * *

Religion is no religion, and virtue is no act of choice, and reward comes by chance and without condition if we only are religious when we cannot choose; if we part with our money when we cannot keep it, with our lust when we cannot act it, with our desires when they have left us.

"Holy Dying," c. iv., sec. 5.

* * *

Let us take care that our religion be like our life, not done like pictures, taken when we are dressed curiously, but looking as the actions of our life are dressed—that is, so as things can be constantly done, that is, that it be dressed with the usual circumstances, imitating the examples and following the usages of the best and the most prudent persons of our communion,

"Ductor Dubitantium," book i. c. vi.

striving in nothing to be singular, not doing violence to anything of nature, unless it be an instrument or a temptation to a vice. For some men mortify their natures rather than their vicious inclinations or their evil habits, and so make religion to be a burden, a snare, and an enemy.

※ ※

It is not enough for a man to be a good citizen unless he be also a good man; but some men build their houses with half a dozen cross-sticks, and turf is the foundation, and straw is the covering, and they think they dwell securely; their religion is made up of two or three virtues, and they think to commute with God, some good for some bad, as if one deadly wound were not enough to destroy the most healthful constitution in the world.

Sermons: "The Righteousness Evangelical," part. iii.

WHAT THE CHRISTIAN RELIGION DOES.

It is a doctrine perfective of human nature, that teaches us to love God and to love one another, to hurt no man, and to do good to every man; it propines to us the noblest, the highest, and the bravest pleasures

"Ductor Dubitantium," book i. c. iii.

of the world ; the joys of charity, the rest of innocence, the peace of quiet spirits, the wealth of beneficence, and forbids us only to be beasts and to be devils ; it allows all that God and nature intended, and only restrains the excrescences of nature, and forbids us to take pleasure in that which is the only entertainment of devils, in murders and revenges, malice and spiteful words and actions. It permits corporal pleasures where they can best minister to health and societies, to conversation of families and honour of communities ; it teaches men to keep their words that themselves may be secured in all their just interests, and to do good to others that good may be done to them ; it forbids biting one another, that we may not be devoured by one another ; and commands obedience to superiors, that we may not be ruined in confusions ; it combines governments, and confirms all good laws, and makes peace, and opposes and prevents wars, where they are not just, and where they are not necessary. It is a religion that is life and spirit, not consisting in ceremonies and external amusements, but in the services of the heart, and the real fruit of lips and hands, that is, of good words and good deeds; it bids us to do that to God which is agreeable to His excellencies—that is, worship Him with the best thing we have, and make all things else minister to it; it bids us to do that to our neighbour, by which he may be better: it is the perfection of the natural law, and agreeable to our natural necessities, and promotes our natural ends and designs: it does not destroy reason, but instructs it in very many things, and complies with it in all; it hath in it both heat and light, and is not more effectual than it is beauteous; it promises everything that we can desire, and yet promises nothing but what it does effect; it proclaims war against all vices, and generally does command every virtue; it teaches us with ease to mortify those affections, which reason durst scarce reprove, because she hath not strength enough to conquer; and it does create in us those virtues which reason of herself never knew, and, after they are known, could never approve sufficiently. It is a doctrine in which nothing is superfluous or burdensome, nor yet is there anything wanting which can procure happiness to mankind or by which God can be glorified: and if wisdom, and mercy, and justice, and simplicity, and holiness, and purity, and meekness, and contentedness, and charity be images of God and rays of divinity, then that doctrine in which all these shine so gloriously, and in which nothing else is ingredient, must needs be from God ; and that all this is true in the doctrine of Jesus, needs no other probation but the reading the words.

REPENTANCE.

That resolution only is the beginning of a holy repentance which goes forth into act, and whose acts enlarge into habits, and whose habits are productive of the fruits of a holy life.

<small>Sermons: "Invalidity of a Late or Deathbed Repentance," part i.</small>

* *

Repentance kills the lust of the eyes and mortifies the pride of life ; it crucifies the desires of the flesh, and brings the understanding to the obedience of Jesus ; the fear of it bids war against the sin, and the sorrow breaks the heart of it ; the hope that is mingled with contrition enkindles our desires to return, and the love that is in it procures our pardon, and the confidence of that pardon does increase our love, and that love is obedience, and that obedience is

<small>"The Doctrine and Practice of Repentance," c. x.</small>

sanctification, and that sanctification supposes the man to be justified before; and he that is justified must be justified still; and thus repentance is a holy life. But the little drops of a beginning sorrow and the pert resolution to live better never passing into act and habit, the quick and rash vows of the newly-returning man, and the confusion of face espied in the convicted sinner—if they proceed no further, are but like the sudden fires of the night, which glare for awhile within a little continent of air big enough to make a fireball, or the revolution of a minute's walk. These, when they are alone and do not actually and with effect minister to the wise counsels and firm progressions of a holy life, are as far from procuring pardon as they are from a life of piety and holiness.

* *

If we refuse to repent now, we do not so much refuse to do our own duty as to accept of a reward. It is the greatest and the dearest blessing that ever God gave to men that they may repent; and therefore to deny it or to delay it is to refuse health brought us by the skill and industry of the physician; it is

Sermons: "The Mercy of the Divine Judgments," part i.

to refuse liberty indulged to us by our gracious Lord. And certainly we had reason to take it very ill if, at a great expense, we should purchase a pardon for a servant, and he, out of a peevish pride or negligence, shall refuse it; the scorn pays itself, the folly is its own scourge, and sits down in an inglorious ruin.

REASON AND FAITH.

He that speaks against his own reason, speaks against his own conscience; and, therefore, it is certain no man serves God with a good conscience that serves Him against his reason. For though, in many cases, reason must submit to faith, that is, natural reason must submit to supernatural, and the imperfect informations of art to the revelations of God, yet in no case can true reason and a right faith oppose each other. "The Worthy Communicant," c. iii. sec. 5.

SCRUPULOUS PERSONS.

They repent when they have not sinned, and accuse themselves without form or matter; their virtues make them tremble, and in their innocence they are afraid; they at no hand would sin, and know not on which "Ductor Dubitantium,' book i. c. vi.

hand to avoid it: and if they venture in, as the flying Persians over the river Strymon, the ice will not bear them, or they cannot stand for slipping, and think every step a danger, and every progression a crime, and believe themselves drowned when they are yet ashore. Scruple is a little stone in the foot—if you set it upon the ground it hurts you; if you hold it up, you cannot go forward; it is a trouble where the trouble is over, a doubt when doubts are resolved; it is a little party behind a hedge, when the main army is broken and the field cleared: and when the conscience is instructed in its way, and girt for action, a light trifling reason, or an absurd fear, hinders it from beginning the journey, or proceeding in the way, or resting at the journey's end.

Let the scrupulous man interest himself in as few questions of intricate dispute and minute disquisition as he can; they that answer fewest, do commonly trouble themselves with most. Curious questions may puzzle every man, but they can profit no man— they are a certain disturbance, they are rebels

Ibid.

in the kingdom of the inner man; they are just the same things in speculation which scruples are in practice, and therefore because notice properly tends and directs to action, the increase of them will multiply these. Avoid them therefore; for not these, but things practical, are the hinges of immortality; but the other break the peace of the superior faculties, they trouble the understanding and afflict the conscience and profit, or instruct no man. He that would cure his scrupulousness, must take care that his religion be as near as he can to the measures and usages of common life.

The scrupulous man is timorous, and sad, and uneasy, and he knows not why. As the melancholy man muses long, and to no purpose, he thinks much, but thinks of nothing; so the scrupulous man fears exceedingly, but he knows not what nor why. It is a religious melancholy; and when it appears to be a disease and a temptation, there need no more argument against its entertainment. We must rudely throw it away.

Ibid.

SECTS.

It is a great fault that men will call the several sects of Christians by the names of several religions. The religion of Jesus Christ is the form of sound doctrine and wholesome words, which is set down in Scripture indefinitely, actually conveyed to us by plain places, and separated as for the question of necessary or not necessary by the symbol of the apostles. Those impertinences which the wantonness and vanity of men hath commenced, which their interests have promoted, which serve not truth so much as their own ends, are far from being distinct religions: for matters of opinion are no parts of the worship of God, nor in order to it, but as they promote obedience to His commandments; and when they contribute towards it, are in that proportion as they contribute parts and actions, and minute particulars of that religion to whose end they do or pretend to serve. And such are all the sects and all the pretences of Christians, but pieces and minutes of Christianity, if they do serve the great end; as every man for his own sect and interest believes for his share it does.

"Liberty of Prophesying," sec. xvi.

The Self-Righteous.

These men are such as think they have knowledge enough to need no teacher, devotion enough to need no new fires, perfection enough to need no new progress, justice enough to need no repentance; and then because the spirit of a man and all the things of this world are in perpetual variety and change, these men decline, when they have gone their period; they stand still, and then revert; like a stone returning from the bosom of a cloud, where it rested as long as the thought of a child, and fell to its natural bed of earth, and dwelt below for ever.

Sermons: "Of Lukewarmness and Zeal," part ii.

Sense.

It cannot be the duty of faith to believe anything against our sense; what we see and taste to be bread, what we see, and taste, and smell to be wine, no faith can engage us to believe the contrary. For, by our senses, Christianity itself, and some of the greatest articles of our belief, were known by them who, from that evidence, conveyed them to us by their testimony; and if the perception of sense were not finally to be relied upon, miracles could never be a demon-

"The Worthy Communicant," c. iii. sec. 3.

stration, nor any strange event prove an unknown proposition; for the miracle can never prove the article unless our eyes or hands approve the miracle; and the divinity of Christ's person, and His mission, and His power, could never have been proved by the resurrection, but that the resurrection was certain and evident to the eyes and hands of so many witnesses. Thus Christ to His apostles proved Himself to be no spirit, by exposing His flesh and bones to be felt: and He wrought faith in St. Thomas by His fingers' ends; the wounds that he saw and felt were the demonstrations of his faith, and in the primitive Church the Valentinians and Marcionites, who said Christ's body was fantastical, were confuted by no other argument but of sense. For sense is the evidence of the simple, and the confirmation of the wise; it can confute all pretences, and reprove all deceitful subtleties; it turns opinion into knowledge, and doubts into certainty; it is the first endearment of love, and the supply of all understanding. From what we see without, we know what to believe within; and no demonstration in the world can be greater than the evidence of sense.

SIN.

A prosperous iniquity is the most unprosperous condition in the whole world.

<small>Sermons: "The Mercy of the Divine Judgments," part ii.</small>

* * *

Let no man despair of God's mercies to forgive him, unless he be sure that his sins be greater than God's mercies.

<small>"Holy Living," c. iv. sec. 2.</small>

* * *

God having appointed for every duty proper seasons and solemnities, hath declared that *he* does his best who heartily endeavours to do the duty in its proper season: but it were well we would remember that he that did a good act to-day can do the same to-morrow in the same circumstances; and he that yesterday fought a noble battle and resisted valiantly, can, upon the same terms, contend as manfully every day, if he will consider and watch. And though it will never be that men will *always* do well as *at some times*, yet when at any time they commit a sin it is not because they could not, but because they would not, help it.

<small>"Unum Necessarium." c i. sec. 4.</small>

* * *

A sinful habit is a state of ungraciousness with God, and sin is possessed of our love and choice. Therefore in vain it is to think a habit innocent because it is a natural product of many single actions. Every proper action of the will is a natural production of the will; but it is nevertheless voluntary. When the understanding hath practically determined the will, it is natural for the will to choose; but yet such a choice is imputable to the will, and if it be not good, is reckoned as a sin. So it is in vicious habits: they are natural effects of many single actions; but then it is also to be remembered that their seat is the will, and whatsoever is naturally there is voluntary still. A habit of sinning cannot remain at all but by consent and by delight, by love and adhesion. The habit is radicated no where but in the will, except it be by subordination, and in the way of ministries. It follows, therefore, that every vicious habit is the prolongation of a sin, a continuing to love that which to love but once is death. For every one that hath a vicious habit chooses his sin cheerfully, acts it frequently, is ready to do it in every opportunity, and at the call of every temptation; and according

Ibid. c. v. sec. 3.

as these things are in every one, so is the degree of his habit. Now since every one of these which are the constituent parts of a habit implies a readiness and apt choice of the will to sin, it follows evidently that the capacity of a vicious habit by which it relates to God, consisting of so much evil, and all of it voluntary upon the stock of its own nature and constitution, is highly and chiefly and distinctly sinful. Although the natural facility is naturally and unavoidably consequent to frequent sinful actions, yet it is also voluntary; for the habit is not contracted, nor can it remain but by our being willing to sin and delighting in the ways of error.

* * *

The dailiness of sin must be bewailed with the dailiness of sorrow. And then "when thou liest down, thou shalt not be afraid; yea, thou shalt lie down, and thy sleep shall be sweet." Now tell me if this balm be not enough to heal the bleedings and bruisings of despair? Talents of sins, and sins in small money, you may hide them all in the wounds of Christ.

"Christian Consolations," c. ii.

The Service of God.

Ecstasies and raptures and conversing with blessed spirits are certainly actions and passions, respectively of greater eminency than dressing the sores of poor boys in hospitals; and yet he that does this serves Christ and does good, while he that follows after the others may fall into the delusions of the devil. That which is best in itself is not best for me: it is best for the best state, but not for the state of men, who dwell in imperfection. Strong meat is better than milk, but this is best for babes; and therefore he would but ill consult the good of his child who, because it is a princely boy, would feed him with beef and venison, wild boar, and the juice of great fishes. Certainly a jewel is better than a piece of frieze; and gold is a more noble and perfect substance than barley: and yet frieze and barley do, in their season, more good than gold and jewels, and are therefore much more eligible. For everything is to be accounted of in its own place and scene of eminency: the eye loves one best, and the tongue and palate, the throat and stomach, love the

marginal note: "Ductor Dubitantium," book iii. c. 3.

other. But the understanding, which considers both, gives the value according to the degree of usefulness, and to the end of its ministry. Now though our understanding can consider things in their own perfections, and proportion honour and value to them, yet that which is better than honour, love and desire, union and fruition, are due to those things most, which, it may be, we honour least. And therefore there are some parts of the service of God which are like meat and clothes, and some which are like gold and jewels; we value and admire these, but we are to choose the other: that is, we prefer one in discourse, and the other in use; we give better words to one and better usages to the other. And therefore those parts of the Divine service which are most necessary, and do most good to mankind, are to be chosen before those that look more splendidly and in themselves import more perfection. The foundation of a house is better than the roof, though the roof be gilded; and that part of the service of God which serves the needs of mankind most is to be chosen before those which adorn him better, so that actions of high and precise religion may be the excellences and perfections of a human soul; but the offices of civil governors, their keeping men in peace and justice, their affrighting them from vile impieties, may do much more good to mankind and more glory to God in the whole event of things.

THE STAR IN THE EAST.

"When they saw the star, they rejoiced with exceeding great joy." Such a joy as is usual to wearied travellers when they are entering into their inn; such a joy as when our hopes and greatest longings are laying hold upon the proper objects of their desires, a joy of certainty immediately before the possession: for that is the greatest joy which possesses before it is satisfied, and rejoices with a joy not abated by the surfeits of possession, but heightened with all the apprehensions and fancies of hope and the neighbourhood of fruition—a joy of nature, of wonder, and of religion.

"The Great Exemplar," part i. sec. 4.

A Remedy for Sadness.

"Sing praises unto God; for it is pleasant." "Sing praises unto our God; for it is pleasant, and praise is comely." "Sing aloud unto God our strength; make a joyful noise unto the God of Jacob." Every furrow in the book of the Psalms is sown with such seeds. I know nothing more certain, more constant, to expel the sadness of the world, than to sound out the praises of the Lord as with a trumpet: and when the heart is cast down, it will make it rebound from earth to heaven.

<small>"Christian Consolations," c. iv.</small>

Temperance.

Sobriety is the bridle of the passions of desire, and temperance is the bit and curb of that bridle; a restraint put into a man's mouth, a moderate use of meat and drink, so as may best consist with our health, and may not hinder but help the works of the soul, by its necessary supporting us, and ministering cheerfulness and refreshment.

<small>"Holy Living." c. ii. sec. 2.</small>

Temperance consists in the actions of the soul principally, for it is a grace that chooses natural means in order to proper and natural and holy ends; it is exercised about eating and drinking because they are necessary, but therefore it permits the use of them only as they minister to lawful ends; it does not eat and drink for pleasure, but for need and for refreshment, which is a part or a degree of need. I deny not but eating and drinking *may be*, and in healthful bodies *always is*, with pleasure, because there is in nature no greater pleasure than that all the appetites which God hath made should be satisfied; and a man may choose a morsel that is pleasant, the less pleasant being rejected as being less useful, less apt to nourish, or more agreeing with an infirm stomach, or when the day is festival by order, or by private joy. In all these cases it is permitted to receive a more free delight, and to design it too, as the less principal; that is, that the chief reason why we choose the more delicious, be the serving that end for which such refreshments and choices are permitted. But when delight is the only end, and rests itself and dwells there long, then eating and drinking is not a serving of God, but an inordinate action, because it is not in the way to that end whither God directed it.

TEMPTATION.

Anything can be done by him that earnestly desires what he ought; secure but your affections and passions and then no temptation will be too strong. Sermons: "Of Lukewarmness and Zeal," part ii.

※ ※

Every temptation puts on its strength as the man is. Sometimes a full meal will not prejudice our health, and at another time half so much would be a surfeit; and some men take cold with leaving off a half-shirt who at another time might leave off half their clothes. The indisposition is within, and if men did not love to be tempted it would not prevail at all. "The Doctrine and Practice of Repentance," c. viii.

※ ※

It is every man's case; trouble is as certainly the lot of our nature and inheritance, and we are so sure to be tempted, that in the deepest peace and silence of spirit oftentimes is our greatest danger; not to be tempted is sometimes our most subtle temptation. "The Great Exemplar," part i. sec. 9.

※ ※

We read a story of a virtuous lady that desired of St. Athanasius to procure for her, out of the number of the widows fed from the ecclesiastical corban, an old woman, morose, peevish, and impatient, that she might, by the society of so ungentle a person, have often occasion to exercise her patience, her forgiveness, and charity. I know not how well the counsel succeeded with her; I am sure it was not very safe, and to invite the trouble to triumph over it is to wage a war of an uncertain issue, for no end but to get the pleasures of the victory, which oftentimes do not pay for the trouble, never for the danger. An Egyptian, who acknowledged fire for his god, one day, doing his devotions, kissed his god, after the manner of worshippers, and burnt his lips. It was not in the power of that false and imaginary deity to cure the real hurt he had done to his devoutest worshipper. Just such a fool is he that kisses a danger, though with a design of virtue, and hugs an opportunity of sin for an advantage of piety; he burns himself in the neighbourhood of the flame, and twenty to one but he may perish in its embraces. And he that looks out a danger that he may overcome it, does as did

Ibid.

the Persian, who, worshipping the sun, looked upon him when he prayed him to cure his sore eyes. The sun may as well cure a weak eye, or a great burden knit a broken arm, as a danger can do him advantage that seeks such a combat which may ruin him, and after which he rarely may have this reward, that it may be said of him, he had the good fortune not to perish in his folly. It is easier to prevent a mischief than to cure it; and besides the pain of the wound, it is infinitely more full of difficulty to cure a broken leg which a little care and observation would have preserved whole. To recover from a sin is none of the easiest labours that concern the sons of men, and therefore it concerns them rather not to enter into such a narrow strait, from which they can never draw back their head without leaving their hair and skin and their ears behind.

A man is sometimes so impressed with the false fires and glarings of temptation that he cannot see the secret turpitude and deformity; but when the cloud and veil is off, then comes the tormentor from within — then the

"Ductor Dubitantium," book i.

calamity swells, and conscience increases the trouble, when God sends war or sickness or death. It was Saul's case when he lost that fatal battle in which the ark was taken. He thought he saw the priests of the Lord accusing him before God. And this hath been the old opinion of the world, that in the days of their calamity wicked persons are accused by those whom they have injured: then every bush is a wild beast, and every shadow is a ghost, and every glow-worm is a dead man's candle, and every lantern is a spirit.

* * *

Epictetus tells us of a gentleman returning from banishment, who, in his journey towards home, called at his house, told a sad story of an imprudent life, the greatest part of which being now spent, he was resolved for the future to live philosophically, and entertain no business, to be candidate for no employment, not to go to the court, not to salute Cæsar with ambitious attendances, but to study, and worship the gods, and die willingly, when nature or necessity called him. It may be this man be-

Sermons: "The Deceitfulness of the Heart," part i.

lieved himself, but Epictetus did not. And he had reason; for ἀπήντησαν αὐτῷ παρὰ Καίσαρος πινακίδες, "letters from Cæsar met him" at the doors and invited him to court, and he forgot all his promises, which were warm upon his lips, and grew pompous, secular, and ambitious, and gave the gods thanks for his preferment. Thus many men leave the world when their fortune hath left them, and they are severe and philosophical, and retired for ever, if for ever it be impossible to return; but let a prosperous sunshine warm and refresh their sadnesses, and make it but possible to break their purposes, and there needs no more temptation; their own false heart is enough; they are like "Ephraim in the day of battle, starting aside like a broken bow."

The Living Temple.

God is especially present in the hearts of His people by His Holy Spirit, and indeed the hearts of holy men are temples in the truth of things, and in type and shadow they are heaven itself. For God reigns in the hearts of

<small>"Holy Living," c. i. sec. 3.</small>

His servants, there is His kingdom. The power of grace hath subdued all His enemies; there is His power. They serve Him night and day, and give Him thanks and praise; that is His glory. This is the religion and worship of God in the temple. The temple itself is the heart of man; Christ is the high-priest who from thence sends up the incense of prayers, and joins them to His own intercession, and presents all together to His Father; and the Holy Ghost, by His dwelling there, hath also consecrated it into a temple; and God dwells in our hearts by faith, and Christ by His Spirit, and the Spirit by His purities, so that we are also cabinets of the mysterious Trinity; and what is this short of heaven itself, but as infancy is short of manhood, and letters of words? The same state of life it is, but not the same age. It is heaven in a looking-glass, dark, but yet true, representing the beauties of the soul, and the graces of God, and the images of His eternal glory, by the reality of a special presence.

Truth.

In the inquiries after truth every man should have a traveller's indifferency, wholly careless whether this or that be the right way so he may find it. For we are not to choose the way because it looks fair, but because it leads surely. _{"Ductor Dubitantium," book i. c. i.}

Virtue.

To love virtue for itself is nothing else but to love it directly and plainly; he that loves it only for the reward, and is not by the reward brought to love the thing, loves not this at all, but loves something else; but he that loves it at all sees good in it because he finds good by it, and therefore loves itself now, whatever was the first incentive: and the wooden arch may be taken away when that of marble is concentred. _{Ibid. book ii. c. i.}

God intends every accident should minister to

virtue, and every virtue is the mother and the nurse of joy, and both of them daughters of the Divine goodness; and, therefore, if our sorrows do not pass into comforts it is beside God's intention; it is because we will not comply with the act of that mercy which would save us by all means and all varieties, by health and by sickness, by the life and by the death of our dearest friends, by what we choose and by what we fear; that as God's providence rules over all chances of things and all designs of men, so His mercy may rule over all His providence.

Sermons: "Miracles of the Divine Mercy," part i.

VIRTUOUS WOMEN.

Virtuous women, like tortoises, carry their house on their heads, and their chapel in their heart, and their danger in their eye, and their souls in their hands, and God in all their actions.

"The Great Exemplar," part i. sec. 2.

Love of the World.

How poor and narrow a heart must that Christian have who confines his love to things present, sweating and toiling for a small part of the goods of this world, which itself is so little! Why doth he content himself with some patch of the earth when he may be lord of the whole heavens?

<small>"Contemplations of the State of Man," c. iii.</small>

* * *

He that is no fool, but can consider wisely, if he be in love with this world, we need not despair but that a witty man might reconcile him with tortures, and make him think charitably of the rack, and be brought to dwell with vipers and dragons, and entertain his guests with the shrieks of mandrakes, cats, and screech-owls, with the filing of iron, and the harshness of rending of silk, or to admire the harmony that is made by a herd of evening wolves when they miss their draught of blood in their midnight revels. The groans of a man in a fit of the stone are worse than all these, and the distractions of a troubled conscience are worse than those groans, and yet a careless, merry sinner is worse than all that. But if we could from one of the battlements of heaven

<small>"Holy Dying," c. i. sec. 5.</small>

espy how many men and women at this time lie fainting and dying for want of bread, how many young men are hewn down by the sword of war, how many poor orphans are now weeping over the graves of their father, by whose life they were enabled to eat; if we could but hear how many mariners and passengers are at this present in a storm, and shriek out because their keel dashes against a rock, or bulges under them; how many people there are that weep with want and are mad with oppression, or are desperate by too quick a sense of a constant infelicity; in all reason we shall be glad to be out of the noise and participation of so many evils. This is a place of sorrows and tears, of great evils and a constant calamity; let us remove from hence, at least in affections and preparation of mind.

WATCHFULNESS.

He that would be free from the slavery of sin, and the necessity of sinning, must always watch. Ay, that is the point; but who can watch always? Why, every good man can watch always; and, that we may not be deceived in this, let us know that the

<small>Sermons: "The Christian Conquest over the Body of Sin."</small>

running away from a temptation is a part of our watchfulness, and every good employment is another great part of it, and a laying-in provisions of reason and religion beforehand, is yet a third part of this watchfulness; and the conversation of a Christian is a perpetual watchfulness, not a continual thinking of that one, or those many things, which may endanger us, but it is a continual doing something, directly or indirectly, against sin. He either prays to God for His Spirit, or relies upon the promises, or receives the sacrament, or goes to his bishop for counsel and a blessing, or to his priest for religious offices, or places himself at the feet of good men to hear their wise sayings, or calls for the Church's prayers, or does the duty of his calling, or actually resists temptation, or frequently renews his holy purposes, or fortifies himself by vows, or searches into his danger by a daily examination; so that, in the whole, he is for ever upon his guards. This duty and caution of a Christian is like watching lest a man cut his finger. Wise men do not often cut their fingers, yet every day they use a knife; and a man's eye is a tender thing, and everything can do it wrong, and everything can put it out, yet, because we love our eyes so well, in the midst of so many dangers, by God's providence, and a prudent natural care, by winking when anything comes against them, and by turning aside when a blow is offered, they are preserved so certainly that not a man in ten thousand does, by a stroke, lose one of his eyes in all his lifetime. If we would transplant our natural care to our spiritual caution, we might, by God's grace, be kept from losing our souls as we are from losing our eyes; and because a perpetual watchfulness is our great defence, and the perpetual presence of God's grace is our great security, and that this grace never leaves us unless we leave it, and the precept of daily watchfulness is a thing not only so reasonable, but so many easy ways to be performed—we see upon what terms we may be quit of our sins, and more than conquerors over all the enemies and impediments of salvation.

DEVOTIONAL BOOKS.

ON THE CATHOLIC FAITH (Notes and Questions). Compiled chiefly from the Works (and in the Words) of the late Rev. E. B. PUSEY. With a Preface by the Rev. T. T. CARTER, Honorary Canon of Christ Church. Second Edition. Fourth Thousand. Crown 8vo, 2s. 6d.

THE GOSPEL AND THE HOME. By CAROLINE M. HALLETT. Readings for Busy People. Crown 8vo, cloth, 2s. 6d.

BY THE REV. CANON JELF.

MOTHER, HOME, AND HEAVEN. Crown 8vo, 5s.

THE SECRET TRIALS OF THE CHRISTIAN LIFE. Crown 8vo. Uniform with "Mother, Home, and Heaven," 5s.

GATHERED FROM THE WRITINGS OF THE LATE REV. E. B. PUSEY, D.D.

A DAILY TEXT-BOOK. By E. H. and F. H. With Preface by the Right Rev. the Bishop of LINCOLN. Square 16mo, cloth, on toned paper, with red lines, 3s. 6d.

HOLY COMMUNION. By E. H. and F. H. (Published by permission.) With Instructions for Holy Communion. With a Preface by the Rev. SCOTT-HOLLAND, Canon of St. Paul's Cathedral. Royal 16mo, limp cloth, 1s. 6d.

PENITENCE. By E. H. and F. H. With a Preface by the Rev. C. W. FURZE, Principal of Cuddesdon Theological College, and Canon of Westminster. Royal 16mo, limp cloth, 1s. 6d.

PRAYERS. Together with others from his Unpublished MSS. By E. H. and F. H. With a Preface by the Rev. R. F. WILSON, M.A., Vicar of Rownhams. Royal 16mo, limp cloth, 1s. 6d.

"PRAYERS," "PENITENCE," AND "HOLY COMMUNION," bound together in One Volume, bevelled boards, with red edges and silk bookmarkers, 4s. 6d.

DEVOTIONS FOR HOLY COMMUNION. Compiled from various Sources. With an Introduction gathered from the Writings of the Rev. E. B. PUSEY, D.D., and a Preface by the Rev. GEORGE E. JELF, Canon of Rochester. 16mo, cloth, 2s.

READINGS FROM THE WRITINGS OF JOHN KEBLE, M.A., and the Rev. EDWARD BOUVERIE PUSEY, D.D. Selected and Arranged by C. M. S. 8vo, cloth, 3s.

A DAILY TEXT-BOOK. Gathered from the "Sermons for the Christian Year," by the Rev. JOHN KEBLE. By E. H. and F. H. With a Preface by the Rev. PETER YOUNG, M.A., Rector of North Witham. Square 16mo, cloth, with red lines, 3s. 6d.; limp purple morocco, red and gilt edges, 10s. 6d.

THE RISE OF CHRISTIAN MONASTICISM. By the Rev. Canon I. GREGORY SMITH. Large crown 8vo, 14s.

CHURCH LORE GLEANINGS. By T. F. THISELTON DYER. Large crown 8vo, Illustrated, 5s.

LONDON: A. D. INNES & CO., 31 & 32, BEDFORD STREET, STRAND.

BOOKS FOR PRESENTS.

THE DAINTY BOOKS.

Each Volume, 2s. 6d.

"Certainly deserve their name. All three are fascinating little volumes, convenient in shape, prettily bound, and charmingly illustrated."—*Athenæum.*

"Dainty" 4to (5¼ by 5), Uniform, Illustrated, Gilt Top.
The Series is intended for children—of *all* ages. Each volume will contain numerous illustrations.

FOR GROWN-UP CHILDREN. By L. B. WALFORD. With Illustrations by T. PYM.

"Bright, graceful, and with a high purpose underlying the dainty trifling."—*Athenæum.*

MUM FIDGETS. By CONSTANCE MILMAN, Author of "The Doll Dramas." With Illustrations by EDITH ELLISON.

"Any little girl would be glad to find a place on her bookshelf for the adventures of Sally and Betty."—*Literary World.*

MASTER BARTLEMY. By FRANCES E. CROMPTON, Author of "Friday's Child." With Illustrations by T. PYM.

"We are glad to speak of this little book with quite unmixed praise."—*Spectator.*

"A very sweet and pure story."—*Academy.*

BROWNIES AND ROSE-LEAVES. By ROMA WHITE. Author of "Punchinello's Romance." Profusely Illustrated by L. LESLIE BROOKE, with Cover designed by the Artist. Large crown 8vo, 3s. 6d.

A RING OF RUBIES. By L. T. MEADE. With Illustrations by L. LESLIE BROOKE. Crown 8vo, 3s. 6d.

DEAR. By the Author of "Tip-cat." Crown 8vo, 3s. 6d.

THE "TIP-CAT" SERIES.

Each Volume uniform, with Frontispiece, crown 8vo, cloth, 3s. 6d.
A Select Series of Books for Girls, uniform in style, binding, and price.

THE HALF-CROWN SERIES FOR ELDER GIRLS.

A well-bound series of copyright Stories by well-known writers, averaging 300 to 400 pages, crown 8vo, 2s. 6d.

THE "YONGE" LIBRARY.

A new, cheaper, and uniform issue of Popular Stories by CHARLOTTE M. YONGE, and other writers, attractively bound in cloth, 200 to 300 pages, royal 16mo, price 1s. 6d. each Volume.

List of Volumes in the above Series post free on application.

LONDON: A. D. INNES & Co., 31 & 32, BEDFORD STREET, STRAND.

Price 40s. the Set of 9 Volumes.

THE READER'S SHAKESPEARE.

A New and Cheaper Issue of this Popular Edition is now ready. Nine Vols. crown 8vo, cloth extra, gilt top, with Portrait.

Single Volumes may be had, price 5s.

Vols. I.-III. contain the COMEDIES.
Vols. IV.-V. contain the HISTORIES.
Vols. VI.-VIII. contain the TRAGEDIES.
Vol. IX. SONNETS, POEMS, and COLLECTED LYRICS.

SOME OPINIONS OF THE PRESS UPON THE FIRST ISSUE.

" Besides being convenient, it is remarkably handsome. For what may be called library use, it is the best Shakespeare we know."—*Guardian.*

" The attempt is very successful. The volumes are of a convenient size, and exceptionally well got up."—*Saturday Review.*

" If any one wishes to read, either for himself or aloud, a play of Shakespeare with pure uninterrupted enjoyment of Shakespeare's genius, he will find this edition the very thing for him. This handsome and unique edition is drawing towards completion, and those who want a copy of Shakespeare for fireside reading will find it everything they could desire. Its convenient size for holding in the hand, its tasteful get-up, its large, clear type, its quasi-antique look and uncut edges, the absence of everything to distract attention from the text, and the general excellence of the text itself, make it at once pleasing to the eye and easy and convenient for continuous reading."—*Scotsman.*

" It promises to be a thoroughly good library edition, and it is certainly cheap."—*St. James's Gazette.*

" It is thoroughly well got up, and may be cordially recommended as a not too expensive library edition."—*Literary Churchman.*

" We feel sure that when this edition is known it will have a wide circulation, and to persons who are intending to get a handsome and serviceable copy of the poet's works, but are puzzled in which edition to invest, we unhesitatingly recommend ' The Reader's Shakespeare.' "—*Sheffield Daily Telegraph.*

" It is a real treasure."—*Church Times.*

" The volumes are of handy size, paper good. The type clear and pleasant to read."—*Evening Standard.*

LONDON: A. D. INNES & Co., 31 & 32, BEDFORD STREET, STRAND.

www.ingramcontent.com/pod-product-compliance
Lightning Source LLC
Chambersburg PA
CBHW020843160426
43192CB00007B/765